DESTINATIONS
UNCOMMON TRIPS, TREKS AND VOYAGES

DESTINATIONS
UNCOMMON TRIPS, TREKS AND VOYAGES

Compiled and Edited by Sonia W. Thomas

Books from
THE CHRISTIAN SCIENCE MONITOR.

Boston, Massachusetts

The articles in this book were originally published
in <u>The Christian Science Monitor.</u>

This book was designed by Taylor and Company,
Boston Massachusetts, in conjunction with Dan
Harvey Graphic Design. This book was designed
and produced on a Macintosh® SE computer using
PageMaker® page layout software (version 3.01).
It was printed and bound in the U.S.A. by Worzalla
Publishing Company, Stevens Point, Wisconsin.

ISBN 0-8750-203-4

Vacations That Test the Skills

Delving Into History

Memorable Voyages

Islands in the Sun

Back to Africa

Closer to Home

Holiday Happenings

The Christian Science Monitor, now in its ninth decade, has always concerned itself with the interests and sights of the entire world. Not surprisingly, the international focus of the newspaper has given rise over the years to many features related to travel. These features have covered destinations throughout the world and included practical suggestions for readers.

In the mid-1930s a regular column entitled Monitor TravelTalk began. This column spurred an increasing number of travel-related stories in the 1940s; in those years prior to the split-second communication of computers and jet aircraft, at least one editor is said to have filed stories by mail from distant locales, pounding out even more features on the long trips home.

More recently, the Monitor has included weekly travel page columns and monthly pullout sections. This coverage earned the Monitor recognition for outstanding travel coverage among newspapers in the United States, as well as awards for section covers and layouts.

The Monitor's pages on travel have included a variety of subjects. Some features have focused on a single locale, offering several articles intended to broaden the reader's overall understanding of the place and its people. Other articles have been more specific in dealing with cruises, budget vacations, and destinations that are particularly remote or exotic. Special activities such as hiking, rafting, skiing, biking and mountain climbing have been included.

This book presents a selection of 50 articles from The Christian Science Monitor, a sampling that highlights some of the topics readers have had fun exploring. These recent articles appeared between 1984 and 1989. And while armchair travelers will certainly enjoy these stories, they also offer practical, updated information for those interested in actually going to any of the destinations.

Special thanks are due each contributor to this book. Further appreciation goes to the many other writers and photographers who shared their travels, and their talents, to make the Monitor's travel pages compelling to readers through the years.

Sonia W. Thomas

Exotic Escapes to the Orient

Memories of a
Pagoda and Peacock Land

Living a Filipino Idyll
at Mrs. Lily B. Luglug's

Monumental Statue Makes
Special Trip Worthwhile

Sampling Samarkand

Malaysia

Daniel B. Wood

MEMORIES OF A PAGODA AND PEACOCK LAND

RAINDROPS FALLING ON LOTUS LEAVES, THE CRUNCH OF MONKS' sandals on gravel paths, and the deep quiet of misty hills—these images from ancient Korea remain seemingly untouched here in this open-air museum.

Far away from the politics and traffic of Seoul and the shipping and auto industries of Pusan, they belong to Kyongju—an area so full of shrines, temples, tombs, gardens, and palaces that UNESCO has designated it one of the world's 10 most important historical sites.

Kyongju will be the prime destination for tourists venturing beyond the capital city. Just about every guidebook calls it the best destination in Korea.

For 1,000 years, it was the capital of the Silla Dynasty, which started here when Julius Caesar was building Rome (57 BC). For nearly 300 years, Kyongju was the capital of the entire peninsula. Overrun by Mongols in the 13th century and then by Japanese in the 16th century, it has been the object of Korea's greatest cultural revival since early in this century.

On a 10-day visit to Korea, my wife and I spent three days wandering the forested mountains, exploring pagodas and temples, locating rock carvings, and deciphering inscriptions with the help of our guide. We came away with great reverence, if not awe, for a history far more vast and complex than America's own.

Besides the natural setting and plethora of historic sites, a national museum caps it all off with art, jewelry, ceramics, and historical exhibits.

1,000 year old Buddha in Sokkuran Grotto.

left: *View of one of the many Kyongju vicinity temples.*

4

North and South Korea, pinpointing Kyongju.

One guidebook says you can spend weeks here and never grow tired of it. I would say four days is the minimum time necessary to take in the major sights, and a week might be better.

There is a small provincial town here, Kyongju City, but we stayed at one of the three resort hotels clustered near the Pomun Lake Resort, about five miles northeast of town. Because the area has long been known as a haven for honeymooners, the hotel was opened in 1978 by the Korean National Tourism Corporation, with an extensive network of shops and recreational facilities and a shuttle to the downtown area.

I have mixed feelings about such calculatedly designed oases of touristdom. But their built-in amenities certainly allow foreign visitors to pay more attention to seeing sights than worrying about logistics.

We arrived in late afternoon, tired from the 4-hour drive from Seoul. With light waning, we decided to start visiting the tourist sights the next morning. We discovered that you can pick your own interests from mammoth lists available at all the hotels. But you will definitely be remiss if you miss any of the following.

Pulguk-sa Temple. The crowning glory of Silla temple architecture, the Pulguk-sa is Korea's most famous temple and my favorite memory of the entire country. I love the abundant use of bright greens, blues, oranges, and reds in the painting on the temple's eaves. Not to mention the sheer numbers of buildings, which take on a majesty when seen together in a visual concert of sloping roofs.

Pulguk-sa is built on a series of stone terraces 10 miles from Kyongju City, in the foothills of Toham-san. Some have called the painting of the interior woodwork, eaves, and massive tile roofs one of the wonders of the world. Built in AD 528, during the reign of King Beobhoung, it was enlarged in 751 but destroyed by the Japanese in 1593. It sat in ruins until 1970, when reconstruction began.

Buddhists at Pulguk-sa Temple participating in a ritual in which they circle a pagoda while praying.

Sokkuram Grotto. The grotto's seated image of the Sakayamuni Buddha was considered the shoreline guardian of the Silla Kingdom. The carving is among the best of dozens of Buddhas we saw on a month-long trip through Japan, Korea, and China, and it is second in elegance, in my mind, only to the Kamakura Buddha in Japan. After parking at a huge mountainside lot, visitors went their way about a mile through woods and up a hill. We made the excursion alone, but were soon joined by no fewer than 60 busloads of schoolchildren. The 8th century grotto that houses the Buddha was made of granite quarried far to the north and transported by mountain path.

National Museum. The grounds are filled with stone remains from the Silla Dynasty, most notably rows and rows of Buddhas, whose heads were broken off during the Japanese occupation.

Trying to photograph ourselves doing the same thing Korean children were doing—placing our heads where the Buddha heads weren't—we were chased away by security guards riding bicycles and blowing shrill whistles. Later, we were virtually attacked by hordes of very young students, who wanted our autographs so they could ogle the funny "foreign" writing.

Many of the stones are carved with relief images of horses, lions, monkeys, and peacocks. And much ado is made over the 23-ton Emille Bell, hanging in a small open-air pagoda of its own. The technique of bronze bell casting is said to have reached its height in the 8th century, and this is the largest and most intricate of them all.

The museum itself is a modern building, and the exhibits don't yet have a permanent feel. This is an indication that the Koreans have only just begun to tap their wealth of history, and archaeology has really been on an upsurge since the Korean war.

Tomb Park. Some 152,000 square meters of landscaping, tomb mounds, and tomb sites were restored by the government between 1973 and 1975. Most tombs date from between the 1st and 4th centuries. Signs lead to the most famous, the Ch'onmach'ong (Heavenly Horse Tomb). Excavated in 1973, the tomb yielded golden jewelry, beads, swords, pottery, gold and silver belts, and bronze shoes.

We enjoyed just walking in the quietude—a somber, if not funereal, atmosphere, punctuated by monks crunching hurriedly down the paths to avoid tourist cameras. Inside one mound, a coffin yielded a painting on birch bark of a flying white horse, considered a great find because of its use as a motif by ancient tribes of northern Asia.

Hiking possibilities abound in and around Kyongju, where the natural scenery is superb. Namsan Mountain is considered one of the best hiking areas.

One of 300 royal tombs in the Kyongju area.

John Edward Young

LIVING A FILIPINO IDYLL AT MRS. LILY B. LUGLUG'S

THE SEVEN-HOUR DRIVE FROM MANILA TO BANAUE WAS ROUGH. Roads in these parts are narrow and winding. And water buffalo keep getting in the way.

These carabao, as they're called here, get off from work early, and tend to slow traffic to their pace as they lumber home down the middle of the road.

Carabao are not the only mode of transport here. Noisy, motorized tricycles dart in and out, and ubiquitous jeepney buses stop to pick up and drop off riders wherever they like.

But the ride seems well worth it, once you make it up the treacherous 45-degree-angle driveway to Lily B. Luglug's Banaue View Inn.

From here, the view of Banaue Village is one of spectacular beauty. This small village, nestled in the shoulder of a mountain in Ifugao Province, is an agricultural wonder of the world.

For more than 2,000 years, Ifugao tribesmen have labored and cultivated the mountainsides into terraced, stone-walled rice paddies. Today, these paddies surround the village like great steps in some giant outdoor amphitheater.

In the darkness of early morning and at dusk, the walls deepen in color, and appear like huge blocks of malachite and mica, reaching from deep in the valley up to the clouds. For nearly 400 square kilometers (150 square miles) they cover the face of the Cordillera Central Mountains.

The stone terraces are considered to be the highest (at 4,000 feet), most

On the road to Lily B. Luglug's Banaue View Inn at the top of the hill.
left: *View of the spectacular rice paddies that surround Banaue Village like a giant outdoor amphitheater.*

8

The Philippines, pinpointing Luzon.

extensive, and best built in the world. Someone has even estimated that, if strung end to end, the terraces would reach more than halfway around the globe—or 10 times as long as the Great Wall of China.

But this is no crumbling monument to the past. The paddies are in fine working order, tended and repaired every day. Women spend long hours bent over, planting and transplanting slender single wisps of rice. Plodding through knee-deep mud, teams of men and carabao plow the terraces. Everyone turns out to help harvest.

Although the rice terraces are what bring the few camera-toting Western tourists to this remote village, there's plenty in town to explore. The roads, however, are little more than stone ruts, so it's best to park your car and lace up your hiking boots. A Banaue tour map should be available wherever you stay, to clue you in to what's ahead as you set out to hike. There's also the Banaue Tourist Information Center, up by the post office, to guide you along.

The best scenery is from Viewpoint, four kilometers (2 miles) out of town on the way to Bontoc. Here an old, skinny, toothless man wearing tribal G-string, cap, and not much else will pose for pictures for a few pesos. That's about as touristy as it gets in these parts.

Banaue Trade Center, a series of shops and restaurants, burned to the ground last year, but still there are enough little shops to poke around in, and even a small market to explore.

You'll find some, what shall we say—"interesting?"— Ifugao art along the way. Like the woven headpieces decorated with tufts of brown and black chicken feathers, and topped with a monkey skull—if that's your style. Beautifully crafted baskets, handsome wood carvings, and fine lost-wax bronze pendants abound. All at fair prices, especially if you bargain. Other shops sell spears and blowguns, more feather and skull headdresses, Ifugao weavings, jewelry, and artifacts.

There are restaurants in town that serve as hangouts for the bearded, sunburned hippie types that find their way to this remote spot in northern Luzon. You'll eat well if you have a particular fondness for chicken or beef curry, carrots, and potatoes.

Be sure to wander up to Bocos Village, just a 10-minute walk from the center of town. You'll meet Mina Plas, a pleasantly roundish woman who sort of resembles the Bloody Mary character in "South Pacific." She's the matriarch of the mini-village and keeper of the rice gods.

These dome-headed, E.T.-esque little carved wooden fellows are kept upstairs in the rice granary. "Oh yes," she may part with one of the male figures— for a price—but certainly not the lone female idol. "Not until my husband carves another," she said, stroking the head of one figure. "That would leave all the men without a woman."

IF YOU GO

Contact the Philippine Dept. of Tourism at 556 Fifth Ave., New York, N.Y. 10036, (212) 575-7915.

Of course if she did sell an idol, "We'll have to sacrifice a chicken," she said. And if reading the entrails suggested the rice gods were not pleased with losing a member, then another chicken, and maybe a pig, would be next on the block.

While Mrs. Plas served us a cup of instant coffee, her two nephews returned from school. They share a hut next door, and they kept quietly busy doing chores—hulling and winnowing rice, feeding mother sow and her five offspring, giving themselves haircuts, and doing a bit of woodcarving to earn extra money.

They care for the chickens too, which nest in covered baskets under the house.

The young boys don't actually live alone. "These are the bones of their grandparents," Mrs. Plas pointed out, as we climbed into their dark hut set on stilts.

The deceased are first buried for a few years, she explained. The bones are then exhumed, polished, and wrapped in fine woven cloth. Of course they are treated with the greatest reverence. In times of family strife, the bones may be unwrapped and repolished, while the deceased's spirit is implored to intercede at a time of trouble.

We waved goodbye to Mrs. Plas, as she reluctantly parted with one of her rice gods and began planning tomorrow night's dinner—fresh chicken. Curry, most likely. And maybe pork after that.

Practical information

Although rare, there are occasional clashes between the communists and local police in these mountains. There is no way to predict these. Apparently, you are relatively safe unless you travel around in a police car! I never met a tourist who was scared off by this, but check ahead with the local police if you are concerned.

The road north of Banaue is just not practical by car, especially in the rainy season. (Friends of mine did it and spent over $1,000 on car repairs.) There are jeepney buses to take you beyond this point.

Good hiking shoes are a must, and a rainproof jacket and sweater. A flashlight comes in handy also. A straight and sturdy walking stick can be picked up along the way to help you clamber over slippery stone terraces.

Don't plan on buying film. If you do find any, which is unlikely, you'll pay dearly.

Young village boy winnowing grain.

Daniel B. Wood

MONUMENTAL STATUE MAKES SPECIAL TRIP WORTHWHILE

THERE ARE LOTS OF REASONS TO TAKE THE ONE-HOUR TRAIN RIDE here from Tokyo: candlelit caves, a lotus lake, peony gardens, the lantern-lined main street. Kamakura is a town as elegant in its contemporary style as it is enchanting, with historic and cultural interest. There are no fewer than 65 temples and 19 shrines in this former seat of shogunate government, now a classy suburb.

But you don't really need any of these reasons beyond the "Daibutsu," the most subtly stirring statue I've seen on a month-long excursion through China, Korea, and Japan.

The Japanese word for "Great Buddha," Daibutsu is a representation of Buddha Amitabha, the Lord of the Western Pure Land, and is worshiped by the great majority of Japanese Buddhists. The statue is so serene in its majesty that it might be best described in poetry, and many have tried. I like this prose description in Bayart Taylor's book, *Japan*: "The Monument… may be considered as the most complete work of the Japanese genius, in regard both to art and to the religious sentiment…a gigantic, seated divinity of bronze, with folded hands, and head gently inclined in an attitude of contemplative ecstasy….There is irresistible charm in the posture…in the harmony of his bodily proportions, in the noble simplicity of his drapery, and in the calmness and serenity of the countenance.''

left: *Daibutsu "Great Buddha"*
a 700-year-old bronze of
enduring religious significance.

12

Japan, pinpointing Kamakura.

The statue was constructed in 1252 at the request of Idanono-Tsubone, a lady attendant of Shogun Yoritomo (1147-1199), who led the nationwide fund raising for the project.

A first image, completed in wood after five years of continuous labor, was destroyed in a storm. The one we see today, measuring 38 feet high and crafted with 93 tons of bronze, was housed in various wooden structures through the years, each destroyed by fire, storm, or tidal wave. Since 1495, the Buddha—hollow as a bell—has stood out-of-doors.

On the way to see the Buddha, I had already fallen in love with Kamakura for everything it was besides a tourist attraction. I found it to be more "real" than, say, Nikko, the resort that forms a backdrop for the great Toshogu Shrine, also a popular day trip from Tokyo. There, besides the wonderful historic sites, you have a tourist-supported community of souvenir shops and seasonal restaurants. But in Kamakura, one finds well-kept neighborhoods, charming restaurants, fine galleries and pastry shops, all of which exist primarily to serve the local population, not tourists.

When you step off the train, you are in the middle of town, with tempting options in every direction. You can take any of a number of short walking tours, with the help of maps provided by local authorities, or you can just browse among the intriguing shops and sights.

Besides the Daibutsu, however, you should not leave town without seeing the great Tsurugaoka-Hachiman Shrine, whose torii gate appears at the north end of Wakamiya-Oji, a main street lined with lanterns, cherry trees, and azaleas. Originally built in 1063 near the seaside town of Yuigaham, the shrine was moved to its present site in 1191 by the first Shogun of Kamakura, Yoritomo Minamoto. Present buildings date from 1828 in the style of the Momoyama period (1573-1602).

About two hours of walking with a numbered map will take you past various shrines, ponds, halls, stones, and gingko and juniper trees. Gravel paths lead through impeccably manicured Japanese gardens and over bridges spanning tinkling streams. Shrines contain armor, masks, and swords from the period when the city was the home of the central government of feudal Japan (1185-1333). Guidebooks relate the significance of the buildings, statues, and paintings produced by artisans from Kyoto and Nara.

There is plenty of history to be found in the small municipal museum, to the right of the shrine, and built in 1928. Memories of the exquisitely carved statues of standing and sitting Buddhas, as well as larger-than-life gatekeepers of hell—all in wood—stand out even after the trip.

The museum, built in the style of the Shoso-in found at the ancient capital of Nara, is an intriguing type of wooden structure that expands and contracts with the humidity, providing its own natural climate control. Adjoining it is Kamakura's Museum of Modern Art, built in 1951, a good stop for visitors who want to see the new as well as the old.

Besides the Daibutsu and Tsurugaoka-Hachiman Shrine, you can follow up your interests to other shrines on the outskirts of the city. Bus and train schedules will help get you to some, though many are within walking distance.

My guide took me to the Zuisenji Temple, a Zen temple of the Rinzai sect with a garden laid out by Muso-Kokushi, considered a famous example of the landscape architecture.

The hillside provides a fabulous view of the entire town, and it contains thousands of miniature, standing marble Buddhas, each representing an unborn child. I also toured the caves nearby—candlelit, musty, with the mood of the burial places they once were.

To the west of town lies a popular seaside resort, Katase. A marineland park is not far away. A wooded island is connected to the mainland by a bridge.

To the southeast, the Miura Peninsula divides Tokyo Bay and Sagami Bay. The nearest town is Zushi, 20 minutes by bus.

Some visitors may want to schedule their trip to coincide with, or avoid, the annual festival of Tsurugaoka-Hachiman Shrine in mid-September (with equestrian and archery contests); Mankakegyoretsu (also mid-September), a masked procession at the Gongoro shrine; and the Kamakura-matsuri (early April) a municipal festival with parades and tea ceremony.

Priscilla Turner

SAMPLING SAMARKAND

TWO RAGGED STONE PILLARS STAND OPEN LIKE JAWS IN THE DRY riverbed near the road. In the old days, camel caravans passed between them on their way to Samarkand. These natural rock columns are called the Gates of Timur, because the 14th-century ruler, Timur the Lame, once extracted tariffs here. Our Intourist bus bumps past them, on a road roughly paralleling the ancient Silk Route.

Soon we're rolling across the open steppe, where cotton and mulberry bushes seem to grow right to the edge of distant, treeless mountains. Women in bright silk harem pants stand apart from men at bus stops.

Here we are—some 2,000 miles southeast of Moscow, in Soviet Central Asia. A Muslim city of 500,000, Samarkand lies about 200 miles from the Afghan border in the Soviet Republic of Uzbekistan. Since extended families live nine or ten to a room in low, shedlike buildings, the city is much smaller than its population would seem to require.

Indeed, Samarkand does not appear large enough to hold all the medieval Islamic monuments and ruins we have come to see. Along the narrow main street, outsize images of Lenin look down at us benignly, the familiar face modified to reflect Central Asian features. Below, street hawkers sell deep-fried meat pies.

Natasha, our urbane, Russian Intourist guide, takes us first to the ruins of

left: *An Uzbek woman in the Silk Routes open-air market.*

Soviet Union near the Afghan border, pinpointing the Samarkand view toward Registan Square.

the Ulughbek Observatory. Ulughbek was the favorite grandson of Timur the Lame, who is known as Tamerlane in the West. Timur may have decreed Samarkand his grand capital, but it was Ulughbek who gave up the life of wars and conquest to make it a center of learning. One story has it that the poet Omar Khayy'am studied mathematics here.

At his observatory Ulughbek achieved a remarkable feat, estimating the length of a year to within 62 seconds of modern-day calculations. Built in 1428, the observatory itself was a wonder, housing a giant marble sextant with a radius of 131 feet and an arc 207 feet long. We look down on the long stone tunnel where the pendulum once swung in the musty coolness; Natasha tells us that Ulughbek was beheaded by his son, who wanted to get on with the business of empire-building.

Ulughbek was eventually buried next to his grandfather at Guri-Emir, a stately mausoleum known for its large and intricately tiled blue-fluted dome, as striking a beacon against the white light of the Central Asian sun as a lighthouse is at sea.

As we enter Guri-Emir's mosaic-covered portal, young Uzbek girls timidly approach, asking us in faulty Russian for gum and souvenirs. Inside, a fledgling contingent of the Red Army, in heavy wool olive-drab uniforms and black boots, listens to a Russian-speaking guide.

Their eyes wander our way over Timur's dark green nephrite tomb. We hear what they hear: that the day after archaeologists opened Timur's graves in June 1941, the Germans invaded Russia, perhaps fulfilling the superstition that led ancient Egyptians to put curses against graverobbers on their hallowed tombs.

Fortunately, modern warfare has never made it as far as Central Asia, and so has never scorched Samarkand's largest and best-known mosques and mausoleums, which have survived countless wars, earthquakes, and neglect. The Soviet government, much to its credit, made it a priority after World War II to restore both Registan Square, at the town center, and the Shakhi-Zinda necropolis, where Muslim pilgrims still come because it is fabled to hold the grave of Kusam ibn-Abbas, Muhammad's cousin.

Shakhi-Zinda is a labyrinth of 20 mausoleums and mosques behind an elaborate towering portal; we stretch to mount the steep, baked brick steps and pass through a small entrance. Bright webs of blue, green, and white cover the mausoleums in patterns of infinite diamonds and stars, their extended lines crossing and recrossing almost as if woven. Natasha tells us that archaeologists haven't found the formula for the unfading cobalt and aqua tiles, which gleam like porcelain in the sun.

Registan Square opens as wide as a fairground, bordered on three sides by madrasahs—Muslim religious schools—of a grand scale. Minarets, domes, and towering lancet arches dating from the 15th to the 17th centuries face off, all decorated in Escher-like mazes of blue tile and majolica. The Sherdor (Lion) Madrasah breaks with Islamic tradition: Its outer portal bears mirror images of a lion chasing a deer, a rising sun rides in the arc of the lion's back with a stylized Asian face peering out from its center.

In a shady corner many feet below, a girl with a glossy black braid that brushes the hem of her tunic is selling lapis lazuli earrings behind a makeshift stand. They cost 35 rubles, almost $60 at the official exchange rate; we settle for terra-cotta dragons for 2 rubles and 35 kopecks.

Natasha wisely advises us to save our money for the open-air market, which spreads itself out behind the ruins of the Bibi Khanym mosque. Once it was a towering affair, among the largest mosques in the Muslim world. The 14th-century architects' imagination exceeded their engineering skill; the mosque fell in almost as soon as it was finished.

Behind wooden counters in the market, Uzbek men size us up over mountains of golden raisins or logs of dense, sticky melon that has been dried and braided, or open cloth bags of spices that would bring a Muscovite to his knees.

I approach a young Uzbek who pretends not to understand my Russian. He takes long sips of tea from a blue-and-white china cup before he finally warms up to me, offering me a sample of his white, creamy honey. I carried his little jar nearly 8,000 miles home. I still haven't finished my Uzbek delicacy.

IF YOU GO

The usual jumping-off point for Samarkand is Tashkent, Uzbekistan's capital, about four hours away by bus. To arrange a tour, contact the Russian Travel Bureau, Intourist, in New York at (800) 847-1800, or inquire at any American travel service specializing in tours of Soviet Central Asia.

Islamic domes and arches mix with postwar Soviet-built housing.

Christopher L. Tyner

MALAYSIA

MY VANTAGE POINT IS A BEACH ON PENANG ISLAND, OFF THE Malaysian Peninsula's west coast. The sun has set over the Indian Ocean, leaving behind a watercolor display. At first, subtle pink, peach, and lavender colors wash lightly over the sky. Then the huge white clouds take on stains of deep gold and orange. Malaysia is showing off.

British novelist and playwright Somerset Maugham, who stayed in Penang when Malaysia played its part in the regal days of the empire, said: "If you haven't seen this place, you haven't seen the world."

But to see this place is one thing; to get there from the United States is another. It took me 21 hours in a 747 jetliner before hometown Boston had spun around to the other side of the world and Malaysia's capital city, Kuala Lumpur, was underfoot.

The map makes it look deceptively simple. The Malaysian Peninsula stretches out south of Thailand and north of Singapore on a long, thin chunk of land that fattens out like one of Popeye's arms. That, together with two states on the north coast of Borneo (400 miles to the southeast, across the South China Sea), makes up the 13-state federation of Malaysia.

But here on the scene, Malaysia turns out to be more tropical and diverse than I had envisioned—a land of friendly people from simple villages and

The Parliament House in Kuala Lumpur.

left: *Top spinning at Cherating Village on Malaysia's east coast.*

20

The Malaysian Peninsula in Southeast Asia.

cosmopolitan cities—surrounded by green mountains and wild jungle and all wrapped in a ribbon of white, sandy beach.

The population of 15 million is a potpourri of Asian culture. With 52 percent of the people Malay, 35 percent Chinese, and 13 percent Indian, the result is a rich variety of life-styles, foods, entertainment, arts, and religions.

This is also a country with a knack for operating in different decades at the same time. I watched a Penang fisherman in his tiny wooden boat hauling in a small catch with his net. Yet a few miles away, an electronics plant was spitting out state-of-the-art computer chips from an assembly line. Intel, Texas Instruments, and National Semiconductor are a few of the American companies that operate here.

On the mainland, in Kuala Lumpur (KL, as locals refer to it), the juxtapositions can be boggling. On an afternoon stroll you might see an old Muslim mosque near a spanking new 50-story office tower; a woman wrapped in an Islamic veil alongside a woman in a smart, gray business suit carrying a briefcase; a wooden shantytown just a short walk from a mirror-walled skyscraper in the business district. Malaysia has one foot planted in the mid-20th century, the other giant-stepping into the 21st. So far it has managed to keep its balance.

East coast

In the sunny life of the fishing villages that stretch the length of the peninsula's east coast, I felt I was peering through an open window on a country's traditional way of life.

In a village north of Kuantan, the fishermen back from their morning's run, dry out their silvery catch under a hot afternoon sun. Their wives boil up some of the fish in large, kiln-like ovens. The children play on rope swings and gawk at the Western tourists who have invaded their village.

Here the population is mostly Malay and Muslim. Even the rooms in the modern, air-conditioned Hyatt Kuantan Hotel have small arrows on the ceiling pointing to Mecca so that the faithful will know instantly in which direction to pray.

All the villages we visited on this coast were similar in many respects. Tiny wooden houses shaded by coconut palms sit within 100 feet of the ocean. The huts are propped about 10 feet off the ground on stilts to keep monsoon floods from invading their living rooms. Outside the front door, just down the stairs, lay piles of coconut husks — the Malay version of insect repellent. While fishing is the dominant trade here, there is some farming of rice, pineapple, and nutmeg.

But the east coast is not all work. It also can show a visitor Malaysia at play. Pastimes such as top spinning, kite flying, shadow play, and folk dancing are must-see attractions.

The tops in use here, made of tin and hardwood, resemble flying saucers 10 inches in diameter. At Cherating, a small coastal village, I watched an elderly Malaysian man wind one end of the thick rope around the top and the other around his wrist, then hurl the top to the ground where it landed spinning. Top spinning is a fine art, and older Malays take the game very seriously. One record spin in the fierce village competitions was recorded at an astounding 1 hour, 47 minutes.

Shadow plays—shows in which flat puppets, usually made of leather, are manipulated out of view of the audience in front of a spotlight that casts shadows onto a white cloth or screen—are a popular form of entertainment. The audience, in front of the screen, watches the shadow characters play out their moral tales. The shows we saw were enchanting.

Downtown Kuala Lumpur, center of the old city.

On the east coast, as well as throughout the Malay Peninsula, there are plenty of modern resort hotels. Most have air conditioning and room service, as well as tennis courts, pools, and sometimes even small workout rooms complete with Nautilus equipment, whirlpools, and saunas. The village of Cherating, however, offers an interesting and inexpensive alternative to city hotels. Here one can live amid Malaysians, just as they do, in locally owned guesthouses that rent for $5 per day (including three meals).

About 25 miles north of Kuantan, one finds a 20-mile stretch of beach (one of only two such in the world) where visitors can observe giant leatherback turtles (some 11 feet long) laying their eggs. Turtle-watching is a nighttime activity from May through September.

Penang Island

Back on Penang Island, where the sunning, swimming, and beachcombing are idyllic, other attractions include the capital city, George Town. One can take a "trishaw"—a tricycle pedaled by a driver with the passenger seat mounted up front—to the lively waterfront and watch the freighters and steamers glide in and out of the harbor. Then one strolls through Jalan Penang, the main shopping bazaar, where electronic gadgets, plastic toys, silks from Thailand and India, fabrics from England, cameras from Germany and Japan, and brocade and sarongs from Malaysia are available at bargain prices.

George Town is also the home of what is said to be the world's third-largest reclining Buddha, measuring 108 feet long and 35 feet high. The Buddha, situated in the Thai Buddhist Monastery, is overlaid in gold, and its giant fingernails are mother-of-pearl.

The Temple of Azure Cloud here is a curious mix: a center of Taoist religious worship and a home for poisonous snakes. The snakes moved in from the outlying jungle long ago, or so the story goes, and have been coming back ever since. Visitors should beware when walking inside the temple, as the snakes have free access to the temple and slither across the floor, on the altar, overhead, and

22

on tabletops. It is said that the fog of incense from the altar keeps them in a drugged state—a story our group desperately wanted to believe.

Kuala Lumpur

Kuala Lumpur got its start as a small tin mining town in 1859. Today it's the center of the nation's government and business. First-class hotels are plentiful, so abundant, in fact, that last year only slightly more than half of the 33,000 rooms were filled. Undaunted, the city is planning to double the number of rooms.

Interesting sightseeing attractions are not quite as common here as throughout other parts of Malaysia, but some are worth noting. Although Malaysia is an Islamic state, not only Buddhists and Taoists, but also Hindus, Sikhs, and Christians, are represented by a variety of shrines, churches, and temples. Kuala Lumpur has two fine mosques: the Jame Mosque, with traditional Arab minarets and domes, and the modern National Mosque, whose marbled hallways can hold 8,000 people.

For a sampling of the nation's history and heritage, the National Museum is a good place to visit. Among its displays are lifelike representations of the Malaysian tiger, the flying fox, and snakes like the cobra and pit viper.

About eight miles north of Kuala Lumpur are the Batu Caves. These huge, cool limestone caverns make a good hike—provided you can pay the steep entry price—272 grueling steps to the top.

Shopping and dining

A popular Malaysian handicraft is Selangor pewter, made from 97 percent tin and 3 percent copper. Vases, mugs, coffee cups, tea sets, and trays are some of the popular pewter items for sale. In Kuala Lumpur, quality and price are regulated by the government, but elsewhere the buyer should beware.

Fairly early in my visit, I reached my limits with the Malay taste for spicy food—chicken curry , beef curry, and crab curry. I sought refuge in a blander Malaysian dish called satay, composed of slivers of chicken or beef barbecued on skewers and dipped in a sweet peanut sauce. Satay can be found at restaurants and open-air food stalls throughout Kuala Lumpur.

Our group also tried a traditional New Year's Chinese steamboat dinner. Ten of us sat around a bubbling pewter bowl filled with a variety of savory fish, accompanied by individual servings of rice.

A Taste of Great Britain

Powis Castle

This Blessed Plot,
This England

The Memory Lingers

There's More to Wimbledon
than Tennis

Bath, England:
Town of Unspoiled Beauty

Christopher Andreae

POWIS CASTLE

WALES IS OVERRUN WITH CASTLES. TO VISIT THIS SMALL COUNTRY without seeing at least one of its hundreds of them is unthinkable. They symbolize its history, its beauty, and even its sadness.

In her 1985 book, *The Matter of Wales,* Jan Morris jocosely characterizes some of them adjectivally.

• Caerphilly Castle, for instance, is "astonishing."

• Chepstow Castle is "brutal."

• Dinefwr Castle: "haunting."

• Cardiff Castle: "exhilarating." Others are "jolly," "domesticated," "silly," or "insensitive."

Powis Castle, just south of the market town of Welshpool, is in the rural county of Powys, mid-Wales. Jan Morris calls it "the most comfortable." Although it began life as a Welsh fortress, she writes, it has been "for 350 years ... a luxurious country residence."

In fact, this red stone castle, its cliff-like walls rising high above steep, terraced gardens, has been continuously inhabited since the last decades of the 13th century. The presumably wooden fortification, which had previously stood

left: *Powis Castle was originally built as a fortress 350 years ago.*

26

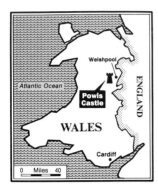

The small country of Wales is overrun with castles.

on the same narrow outcrop, had been destroyed in one of the repeated skirmishes between the Welsh princes in this border area. Its owner, for good or ill, had formed an alliance with the nearby enemy, England.

Thanks to this alliance, the stone castle was subsequently built. It has been altered and enriched over the centuries since, but still retains externally the air of a 13th-century fastness. Its owner, Gruffyd ap Gwenwynwyn, was given back his possessions by English King Edward I, when Edward at last managed to subdue Wales.

Comfort in an ancient castle must be rather a relative term, but the visitor to Powis today feels a grandeur warmed and softened by centuries of family living. Even now, with Britain's National Trust running Powis, making many of its attractions accessible to tourists, the current (sixth) Earl of Powis still lives here. The trust specializes in this kind of arrangement for its properties, and often achieves a remarkable balance between their private and public character as a result.

The trust's administrator at Powis, Major Neville Williams, showed us around. He led us up the grand 17th-century staircase into the library, the blue drawing room, the "gateway room," and the oak drawing room. He commented fluently on works of art, furniture, Mortlake tapestries, ceiling paneling, murals, family portraits, and Indian relics. The last are from the collection of Lord Clive of India, whose son married a Powis heiress in 1784 and later became Earl of Powis.

Two portraits indicated by our guide were of Clive's daughters. They were by the delightful 18th-century portraitist George Romney. Joshua Reynolds's fine skills are also represented by a portrait of Lady Henrietta Herbert. This Countess of Powis, living until 1830, was a descendant of the Sir Edward Herbert who had purchased the castle during the reign of the first Queen Elizabeth in 1587.

Dreamlike, visionary painting

The castle's most remarkable picture is also of a Herbert. Protected in a glass case, this small, sparkling gem of a painting, dreamlike and visionary, is Isaac Oliver's 17th-century miniature on vellum of Lord Herbert of Cherbury, brother of George Herbert, the metaphysical poet.

In the blue drawing room Major Williams drew particular attention to a pair of 18th-century black lacquer commodes—English, with Japanese panels. Dating from the 1760s, they are attributed to Pierre Langlois.

Looking through one of the many windows (which from the outside break up and humanize the defensive façades of the castle), he told us that some of the walls are 13 feet thick. Their red gritstone was quarried here. Nearby landmarks include the River Severn; Britain's tallest tree; and Offa's Dyke, the 8th-century entrenchment marking the boundary between Anglo-Saxon and Welsh territory. To the northeast are the Breidden Hills.

Some of the upstairs windows look over the remarkable terraced gardens sloping southward from the house. The white figures of shepherds and shepherdesses on the balustrade above the orangery are, he told us, actually made of lead. They had recently been painted white to look as they would have originally: a cheap substitute for marble. The rustic elegance of these rare pieces is, in fact, a charming feature of what basically are formal gardens.

These gardens vie with the house for visitor appeal. Thought to have been laid out in the late 17th century, they withstood—apparently through neglect rather than a deliberate effort—all the dangers of "improvement" common in British country-house gardens through the 18th century, often at the hands of "Capability" Brown. He, given the chance, would have informalized them. Instead they have kept a distinct period flavor and are reminiscent of Italian Renaissance terraced gardens.

Rich Elizabethan plasterwork

Their powerful regularity and geometry have, all the same, been allowed to mellow over the years. Flowers climb, hang, and festoon the terraces, clothing the severity of the stonework. The enormous yew hedges are possibly the most unusual development of all. They billow up almost like dark clouds, strange amorphous masses of green. Over the centuries they have achieved a scale commensurate with the castle itself. It is hardly surprising that W. Robinson, the vigorous exponent in the 1880s of "the wild garden," said few gardens gave him more pleasure than Powis.

But Powis as a whole is not unused to praise. And two of its finest rooms were still waiting for us: first, the "long gallery." Long galleries were much more than passages. They were for weatherproof exercise and display of pictures, tapestries, furniture, and sculpture. Mark Girouard has called Powis's, formed at the end of the 16th century by Sir Edward Herbert, "one of the most evocative of Elizabethan long galleries." He relishes its "wonderful, rich Elizabeth plasterwork."

Major Williams then took us into the oddest room in the castle, the state bedroom. This opulent, though not enormous, 17th-century room intrigues architectural historians. Richly gilded balusters cross the room. A portion of the balusters swings open like a garden gate to give access to the tapestry-surrounded bed. Crowns and the initials CR indicate its royal function. Experts seem to agree that the king in question was not, as traditionally thought Charles I, but his son, Charles II. That the Herberts were ardent Royalists is well known. Their allegiance had provoked an invasion of the castle during the civil war by Cromwell's parliamentary troops and resulted in temporary exile for the Herberts. But at the second Charles's restoration in 1660, they were reinstated.

IF YOU GO

Powis Castle and Garden are open to the public Wednesday through Sunday after March 24 and in April, May, June, and September, Wednesday-Sunday, 12 to 5 p.m. In July and August, the garden is open daily from 11 a.m. to 6 p.m., and the castle, Tuesday-Sunday, 11 a.m. to 6 p.m. It is open on Sundays only in winter.

Patricia A. Taylor

THIS BLESSED PLOT, THIS ENGLAND

IT'S ENCOURAGING TO KNOW THAT THREE OF ENGLAND'S GREATEST gardens were created largely by amateurs.

Great Dixter in E. Sussex, Sissinghurst in Kent, and Hidcote in Gloucestershire consist of a series of outdoor "rooms." These are relatively small spaces enclosed by green hedges or rustic stone walls and filled with groupings of colorful flowers and shrubs.

The overall settings are spectacular. But because the gardens consist of manageable divisions, they offer practical suggestions for those with even the tiniest of flower beds. All provide sumptuous scenery for gardeners and non-gardeners alike.

Great Dixter, eight miles northwest of Rye, is still being fashioned by Christopher Lloyd, one of its creators. Mr. Lloyd is a connoisseur collector of plants who loves to test new hybrids and play with color combinations. This gardener is also a premier writer, describing his garden's triumphs and failures in books, columns, and articles.

Great Dixter's design was laid out almost 80 years ago by Edwin Lutyens, a turn-of-the-century architect whose influence on garden structure is still felt today. At the time Sir Edwin began to practice, garden style dictated vast panoramas of field and woodland.

Hidcote's raised pool is a special delight.

left: *Two topiary birds invite visitors into Hidcote's fusia garden.*

He proceeded to reduce this scope and reintroduced the concept of formal design, using the roomlike divisions that had been popular from Roman through Tudor times. In doing so, he made it possible for those with smaller plots of land to aspire to artistic achievement in the garden.

At Great Dixter, Lutyens laid out 18 distinct compartments. These were filled with topiary, a typical accompaniment to a "room garden," and then planted by Lloyd's mother. It was she who filled one "room" with antique roses and who had young Christopher help her plant the meadow garden with a splash of bulbs and wildflowers.

While Lloyd has left some of his mother's plantings intact, other "garden rooms" at Great Dixter form a hot house of horticultural experimentation. This laboratory aspect can best be appreciated in the famous Long Border, a brilliant tapestry of plants measuring 70 yards in length and five in depth.

Best seen from the month of June on through the summer months, this magnificent garden planting is an ever-changing, riotous color mixture of perennials, annuals, bulbs, small shrubs, and even trees—something to be seen!

In contrast to the evolving plantings at Great Dixter, those at Sissinghurst— less than an hour's drive to the northwest—are a static but living monument to Vita Sackville-West and Harold Nicolson.

The diaries and letters of this couple (particularly as depicted in the book *Portrait of a Marriage*) have chronicled their nontraditional, but highly cultured and literate lives. However, their petty affairs can be boring and make one wonder what was so special about this man and woman.

A visit to Sissinghurst supplies the answer. It is a stunning work of art, created by two individuals who had no formal horticultural training.

They acquired Sissinghurst in 1930. It consisted of some ruined buildings and rubbish-strewn fields. "I saw what might be made of it," Sackville-West wrote. "It was Sleeping Beauty's garden…a garden crying out for rescue." The two were to spend the next 30 years answering that cry.

Nicolson designed the garden, and she planted it. He favored the formal approach advocated by Edwin Lutyens (a close friend of his mother-in-law), and created an austere geometric layout. He extended the concept of "room gardens" and used borders of clipped boxwood hedges to create "rooms" within "rooms" in many of the nine garden spaces.

Sackville-West then gave full play to her romantic impulses in planting her husband's design. She copied the old cottage garden style—lush, crowded arrangements of many different flowers—and added the idea of themes. Thus, she created the White Garden, described as "the most beautiful garden at Sissinghurst, and indeed of all England." Every flower in this garden—fragrant roses, woolly lambs' ears, dusty millers, and many more—is either white or gray.

right: *Massed daffodils at Sissinghurst.*

Each "room" has its own special motif. In early spring, for example, the Lime Walk is garishly filled with the reds, blues, yellows, and whites of daffodils, forget-me-nots, anemones, and bluebells. This part of the garden then rests while others—such as the herb and rose gardens—come into their own in the warmer months.

Sackville-West was protective of Sissinghurst. When it was first proposed in 1954 that she give the garden to the National Trust, she vehemently wrote in her diary, "Never, never, never!" But when she died in 1962, the family couldn't afford to pay the estate taxes, and the property came under Trust auspices.

The enigmatic creator of Hidcote, Lawrence Johnston, on the other hand was the first person to donate such a property to the National Trust. He did so in 1948, packed up his baggage and his dachshunds, and moved to southern France, leaving England and his magnificent garden forever.

Mr. Johnston is always referred to as "the American," but he was so in parentage only. He was born and raised in Paris, and attended Cambridge University. Johnston became a British citizen in 1900 and acquired Hidcote in 1907, when he was 36.

There was nothing surrounding the hilltop Cotswold mansion, 35 miles

Hidcote's Pillar Garden is enclosed by stately manicured yews.

northwest of Oxford, but simple farm land. Out of this, Johnston fashioned a masterpiece.

One of Hidcote's charms is that individual flower varieties are planted in small groups and then surrounded with grandiose atmospheres. Thus, the Pillar Garden is enclosed by immense sculptured pillars of yew, while one of its borders is a simple mixture of mock orange shrubs, purple lavender, and yucca plants.

As Sackville-West wrote in 1949, the 21 or so gardens at Hidcote appeal "alike to the advanced gardener in search of rare or interesting plants, and on the aesthetic side to the mere lover of beauty." Where Johnston got his ideas from and why he implemented them as he did are mysteries.

He had money, which always helps. And as his passion for gardening grew, he became more knowledgeable—going on plant expeditions to South Africa in 1927 and China in 1931, and creating his own hybrids, such as Hidcote Lavender. Though he treasured, indeed insisted upon his privacy, he entertained many of the *beau monde*. He is supposed to have designed Edith Wharton's Paris garden.

Under National Trust sponsorship, Hidcote's beauty is scrupulously maintained. In addition to its exotic topiary and theme borders, it features sweeping lawns, meandering streams, brick walks, a raised pool, and cozy gazebos. From spring through fall, there is always something of interest for even the most casual of visitors. It is somewhat ironic, however, to realize that this grandest of English "room gardens" was created by a man with an American inheritance and a French background.

Each garden is an easy day trip from London and best reached by car. A road atlas is most helpful in plotting a route. Signs are posted near each location, and pedestrians are quite willing to help with instructions. For the most current information on fees and opening times, buy a copy of the 1990 edition of *Gardens of England and Wales* (known as the "Yellow Book") for £1 upon arrival in England. This handy reference tool, available in most bookstores, provides detailed information on over 2,300 private gardens.

Great Dixter is in Northiam, about 8 miles northwest of the seacoast town of Rye.

The garden is a private one. There are parking and restrooms, but no refreshments. There are separate charges to see the gardens and the mid-15th-century farmhouse.

Sissinghurst is located in the heart of Kent, near a little town called Cranbrook. As a National Trust property, it offers a pleasant lunch and tearoom, a gift shop, restrooms, and a parking lot.

Hidcote is near Chipping Campden, about 35 miles northwest of Oxford and 12 miles south of Stratford-upon-Avon. It features the same amenities as Sissinghurst.

IF YOU GO
The British Tourist Authority will supply a map showing notable gardens in Great Britain. Call (212) 581-4700 in New York City.

David Butwin

THE MEMORY LINGERS

IN THAT LIVING, CHANGING THEATER THAT IS LONDON, A CERTAIN few figures from the past demand center stage. One can readily see Dickens here and there, and Queen Victoria and Christopher Wren are highly visible, but perhaps no one plays a more pervasive role than Winston Spencer Churchill. For me, Winnie is everywhere.

Churchill will have been gone 25 years in January 1990, and later this year it will have been 45 years since he saw Britain through the end of World War II. Yet even today it is not hard to conjure up the image of the ever-hopeful prime minister striding through the bomb-torn city, raising two fingers for victory. For more tangible evidence there are busts or statues at St. Paul's, Parliament Square, and Guildhall, but perhaps the most novel memorial is an underground warren of rooms on Great George Street near Whitehall.

These are the Cabinet War Rooms, used as a hideaway by Churchill, his war cabinet, and the chiefs of staff during the bleakest days of the war. In 1981 the rooms, scarcely altered from their wartime use, were turned into a museum, and a well done one at that. On sunny days when half the world seems to be thronging the Tower of London, Westminster Abbey, and Madame Tussaud's, this subterranean retreat is orderly and quiet.

One needs the resourcefulness of a secret agent or at least the pluck of a

left: *Roberts-John statue of Churchill (unveiled in 1973) overlooks the Houses of Parliament.*

The Map Room as it appeared in 1945.

seasoned tourist to find the museum. Having consulted at least two bobbies, I finally found the hidden steps and soon was 10 feet below the pavement and heading back over 45 years in time. The Cabinet War Rooms are the surviving and most significant part of underground emergency accommodations the British built to protect their leaders in the threatening days just before the war. The hideout was chosen for its proximity to Whitehall and for the extra security offered by the steel-framed structure of the building above.

Starting along the maze of narrow corridors, one comes first to the Cabinet Room, which was used 100 times by Churchill, his war cabinet, and defense committee between 1940 and 1945. They were driven underground most frequently during the blitz of September-November 1940 and four years later when the Germans raked London with a V-rocket offensive.

You look through a glass panel at a room arranged to look as it did for a meeting on Oct. 15, 1940, at the worst of the blitz. A clock on the wall reads a few minutes to 5. At the center of the 30-by-30-foot room is a horseshoe-shape table covered with somber navy blue cloth. Around it are 23 chairs, including a wooden swivel chair favored by Churchill, who sat before a large pull-down map of the world. There are electric fans in each corner, and above the door are two small electric bulbs, one red and one green, to indicate whether an air raid was in progress.

Along the main corridor you pass a hatchway leading to a subbasement where many of the staff slept during the worst bombing raids, a mess room, and a weather board, which was occasionally marked "windy" during air raids—a joke to keep spirits buoyed.

One of the most vital chambers is a phone room Churchill used to speak directly to President Roosevelt in the White House. On a desk beside a green-shaded lamp are the earphones Churchill used for those conversations. Throughout the war, devices called scramblers were used to transform conversations into meaningless noise; then the words were unscrambled on the other end. An airtight link did not exist between this room and Washington until mid-1943, when the Bell Laboratories developed an advanced scrambler. It was too large for the Cabinet War Rooms, though, and had to be installed in the basement of Selfridge's department store on Oxford Street and connected to the phone room by underground cable. I had to chuckle at the thought of all the meaningless noise going on at that very moment in Selfridge's basement, at the peak of London's July sales.

As I passed a series of rooms, each equipped with typewriters, desks, sleeping cots, and World War I iron helmets hung on wooden posts, I found myself listening to the comments of an English threesome—presumably grandmother, daughter, and granddaughter. "Sugar was rationed in those days," said the grandmother, "and I remember we could only get three-and-a-half bottles of milk a week."

"Goodness, we have 18 delivered now," said the mother. Added the eldest: "And we could buy a half leg of lamb once every fortnight." The youngest, perhaps 10, merely gazed on the displays.

In the Map Room you see the very wall maps used at the end of the war, with a series of pins showing the movements of convoys and individual warships. Churchill's private room is next to the Map Room, furnished with a cot covered with a greenish quilt, a floor heater, and a large map of the area between London and the Suez, partly concealed by half-drawn curtains. Churchill slept here only three times during the blitz—he found the toilet facilities inadequate—and after December 1940 he and Mrs. Churchill lived in private apartments upstairs on the ground floor. He did make a number of telling broadcasts from the dungeon room in 1940—an invasion warning on September 11, and a broadcast to the French on October 21.

I tracked the Churchill presence elsewhere in London, realizing that one cannot enter St. Paul's, for example, which he ordered preserved through the bombing, without recalling his—and the church's—indomitable wartime spirit. My favorite memorial, though, is the Churchill Room of the Jermyn Street shirtmakers, Turnbull & Asser. Churchill was a longtime customer, and in a glass cabinet resides a green velvet siren suit he wore in the war rooms. Even in the darkest hours, Sir Winston went in style.

Churchill's wartime underground Cabinet Room.

Constance E. Putnam

THERE'S MORE TO WIMBLEDON THAN TENNIS

YOU DON'T HAVE TO PLAY TENNIS OR CARE ABOUT WATCHING those who do to enjoy a visit to Wimbledon, site of the annual tennis championships held each June.

While "Wimbledon" is synonymous with "tennis" to many people—and rightly so—the town has more to offer travelers than its fabled courts.

Many English towns have shops and restaurants that make them attractive to visitors, but few are as accessible from the center of London as Wimbledon. An easy "underground" ride on the District Line will take you to Wimbledon Station. Or a faster way is to take a British Rail train from Waterloo Station.

Once you arrive at the underground station, you are squarely in Wimbledon's bustling, modern section, new by English standards, since it grew up in the late 19th century when the railroad was built. Until nearly modern times, there was nothing here except fields.

Wimbledon Village is up the hill. In sharp contrast to the area around the station, the village has medieval origins. And, although the old manor house is long since gone, there is technically still a lord of the manor of Wimbledon—none other than Earl Spencer, father of the Princess of Wales.

The walk up Wimbledon Hill Road to the village is too steep to appeal to everyone. But buses run frequently, and only in a downpour will you have to wait

left: *Cozy shops on Wimbledon's High Street.*

40

The Brewery Tap is one of many quaint English pubs in the village.

long for a London cab. The way up the hill takes you past department stores, restaurants, private homes, the post office, the library, a greengrocers with a handsome display of cut flowers and produce, and even a shop that purports to sell 31 flavors of genuine American ice cream.

At the top of the hill, passing the stone memorial to one Joseph Toynbee, Esq. FRS, you're ready for a stroll along High Street, the main thoroughfare. Here you'll find more places to eat. Most notable, perhaps, is the dramatic increase during the last couple of years in the number of establishments serving afternoon tea. The Coffee Shop and Anabel's Salon de Patisserie now compete with the Forget-Me-Not Tea Room farther along.

Next to Gravestock's Bakery there's also Gravestock's Sandwich Shop, complete with "take away" options. And restaurants of various sorts abound.

About midway along High Street, a sign points off to the right announcing the "Lawn Tennis Museum at the All England Club." "St. Mary's Parish Church" is also signposted there. And in fact, the church is worth a detour. Today's building is on the site of a much older church, which, with a few houses along what was then known simply as "The Street," *was* the medieval village of Wimbledon.

While you are exploring this section, you may want to look at a few side streets. Each one is different, but they all look wonderfully English to American eyes. The half-timbered houses and the prevalence of brick—there are very few frame houses—are further English cues. So is the fact that virtually every house, no matter how small, has its garden. And, although many gardens are walled, the bright profusion and perfume of flowering trees and other blooms cannot be kept hidden altogether.

Longtime residents find High Street today not what it used to be, and they regret some of the changes. There is no question that the influx of shops like the Real Cheese Shop, with its elegant presentation of more than 140 cheeses, is indicative of a definite move up-market. Still, for the visitor it is lovely.

Even so, other English villages have their shops, restaurants, charming houses, and parish churches. And many trace their history to medieval times. But what makes Wimbledon unique, apart from the tennis, is Wimbledon Common, an expansive refuge of greenery that opens out before you at the end of High Street, just past the war memorial. Together with Putney Lower Common, Wimbledon Common comprises 1,100 acres, measuring more than a mile and a-half on each of its four sides.

If you're tired of city pavements, you can leave macadam behind here and ponder an earlier England. This common was once the site for some famous duels. In 1798 Prime Minister William Pitt dueled George Tierney here.

For London visitors who have no time for an extended trip into the English countryside, Wimbledon Common may be just right to capture some of the country's rural flavor. Kite flying, dog walking, outings, and games are the pastimes here.

Crisscrossing pedestrian paths, "roads," and riding trails cut through most sections of the Common. Golf courses, playing fields, and sports grounds also break up the open areas and deeply wooded sections.

A good map of the Common, available from the local bookshops, is likely to prove useful to anyone spending some time here. Special points of interest, such as the windmill in the northern corner, are clearly marked, as is Caesar's Camp, a 14-acre area thought to be the remains of earthworks from the New Stone Age.

Follow the road from the windmill to Cannizaro Park, and you'll find a fine old estate, Cannizaro House, that has been turned into a hotel. The gardens, which are open to the public, offer carefully tended flower beds, towering rhododendrons, sweeping lawns, and magnificent trees. When you leave Cannizaro Park, it's worth pausing for a moment where West Side Common and Southside Common come together. Fronting on a tiny green is Crooked Billet, as quaint a street as you could ask for.

By then, it may be time to head back to the station. After such a day, you'll be able to tell friends that you were *in* Wimbledon. Maybe they'll notice a distinction from the tennis crowd, who usually say they were *at* Wimbledon.

IF YOU GO

For more information, contact the British Tourist Authority at 40 W. 57th St., New York, NY 10019, (212) 581-4700.

The grand Cannizaro House offers wonderful gardens with sweeping lawns in its park.

Kristin Helmore

BATH, ENGLAND: TOWN OF UNSPOILED BEAUTY

TO MANY TRAVELERS, ONE OF THE DELIGHTS OF A COUNTRY LIKE England is its manageable size. You can journey from London to almost any corner of the kingdom in less than a day. Trains are excellent, and there are even some super-speedy ones that hurl you through the landscape at 125 m.p.h.

This service is called the "1-2-5," and it will get you to Edinburgh or Glasgow in just a few hours. Or, if your stay in England is very short, and you feel you can only manage a day-trip out of London, one of the loveliest—and easiest—places to visit is Bath.

If Bath conjures up images of 18th-century dandies, women in sedan chairs arriving at the Pump Room, or lovingly excavated Roman ruins, you won't be disappointed. But if you imagine, as I did, that by now Bath has become just another modern city with a few historic points of interest, you will be in for a delightful surprise. This little city seems so unspoiled that you feel Jane Austen herself could stroll down Milsom Street today, or climb the hill to Lansdown Crescent, and feel perfectly at home.

left: The town's 2,000 year old Roman baths are still intact.

Pulteney Bridge, Bath, England was built in 1770 and is lined with shops.

If you catch the 1-2-5 at Paddington Station, London, at about 10 in the morning, as we did, you can enjoy a delicious English breakfast on a thick white linen tablecloth served by a liveried waiter, as the rich and varied greens of the English landscape glide swiftly by out the window. In an hour and five minutes, you're in Bath; it almost seems too soon.

Even before you arrive, though, you are aware of one of the special qualities of this western part of the country. The villages are built with a warm, golden-colored stone, which glows against the deep greens of fields and trees. And as you pull into Bath Spa station, you find the whole city comfortably spread on a hill before you. This is your first indication that Bath has not been spoiled by the 20th century: the whole town seems to be built of that wonderful, honey-colored "Bath stone."

To plant yourself firmly in history, a few steps from the station will take you through the Roman thermae of Aquae Solis (the Latin name for Bath, after the goddess Sul Minerva, patroness of wisdom, arts, science, and war). Here the hot sulfur springs, for which the city is named, still bubble up at the rate of six gallons a second, as they have for centuries. The Romans were only among the first of a long line of aristocrats who flocked to Bath through the ages, to drink and bathe in these waters.

The entrance to the Roman Museum is in the delightful little square facing the cathedral, Bath Abbey. And you can walk right out of the enclosure of the huge Roman bathing pool—which is still fed from the hot springs through a 2,000-year-old lead pipe—into the elegant 18th-century Pump Room.

Dickens in *The Pickwick Papers* makes you expect something much larger, as it is clear that in his day everybody who was anybody congregated there every morning to see and be seen, and generally to outdo each other in their displays of finery. They also took a drink from the pump, which looked a bit like a large baptismal font to me. Sam Weller, Pickwick's stand-up comic of a servant, remarked that the water tasted like "warm flat-irons." A great deal went on in this room in English social history, as in English literature. Could it be that even the flat, slip-on shoes worn by those well-dressed crowds around the turn of the 19th century took their name from the Pump Room, coming down to us as pumps?

You emerge from the Pump Room into Abbey Yard, with baskets of flowers hanging around you from a graceful open arcade. The scale is small — designed for strolling, gossip, people watching. Jane Austen fits in perfectly.

There had been an Abbey on the present site, built right into the Roman ruins, since at least the 10th century. The present version of it was begun in the 15th century. Known as the Lantern of the West because of its many windows, it is a delicate and ethereal late-Gothic building. To me, its most charming feature was the double relief of Jacob's Ladder, with angels ascending and descending (in

right: *It's Roman ruins and 18th-century flavor are just an hour from London.*

46

IF YOU GO

The British Rail will give more information about train trips to Bath that run hourly and cost $88.00 1st class, or $60.00 2nd class. Call (212) 682-5150 in New York City.

The ancient Roman built bathing pool is still fed to this day from the hot sulfur springs through a 2,000-year-old lead pipe.

very human, rather clumsy and endearing postures) up and down the twin bell towers of the façade.

Through the portico opposite, you find yourself on a street with no cars — only attractive, venerable little shops, leisurely strollers, and hanging flower baskets at every turn. As you start up the hill, this becomes Milsom Street, and you can easily imagine the military heroes of Jane Austen's *Persuasion* escorting their women up and down this elegant little thoroughfare.

Almost all the buildings you see in Bath are from the 18th century, in an understated, delicate English version of the Greek-inspired Palladian style, perfected by John Wood, Thomas Baldwin of the Adam school, John Palmer, and others.

The ultimate examples of the Bath style are found in the various residential circuses, squares, and crescents, where graceful, unbroken sweeps of uniform townhouses preserve the stately elegance of the period.

The Circus, where Gainsborough and Wordsworth both lived, is a generous, continuous circle of these fashionable homes, with a round green lawn and a thick clump of trees in the middle.

Royal Crescent is even more impressive. In one of the corner houses is the Bath Historical Society, whose rooms have been completely restored in 18th-century style: wallpaper, rugs, table settings, prints, paintings, and all.

The Assembly Rooms, a building designed by John Wood in 1770, contains a number of elegant rooms for concerts and social gatherings. These have been authentically decorated in the colors and with some of the furnishings of the period. You can have a light lunch of sandwiches and tea in one of these rooms, followed, perhaps, by a shiny sweet roll with sugar and currants on top: what the English call a "Bath bun."

You can really get a feel for the look and atmosphere of Bath in just a day of strolling up its sloping streets. And a worthwhile objective of your climb could be the famous Lansdown Crescent, which rests on the brow of the city like a tiara, offering a magnificent view of the rolling emerald countryside below.

Designed in the 1790s by John Palmer, Lansdown Crescent seems to distill the essence of Bath's restrained and elegant style. The gentle curve of the houses is set well back from the road and they can be approached only across a generously wide sidewalk. Many of the houses have their original wrought-iron lampholders arching before their doorways.

Bath seems rather quiet these days. You feel that lovers of art, culture, and history must live there, faithful to the memory of Sul Minerva. The residents obviously take pride in the unique, unspoiled beauties of their town. Maybe they commute to London on the 1-2-5. It's easy enough: We got back that evening in time for dinner and the theater.

Train Journeys
Recapture the Past

From the North Woods to the Rockies,
the Railway Lets You Swallow
North America Whole

A Ride on the Modern-Day Orient Express
Recalls an Era of Opulence

The Night Train to Victoria Falls

A Rail Pass Puts Europe at Your Feet

On the Tracks of Marco Polo

William G. Scheller

FROM THE NORTH WOODS TO THE ROCKIES, THE RAILWAY LETS YOU SWALLOW NORTH AMERICA WHOLE

THEY STOOD AT A LONELY SPOT CALLED CRAIGELLACHIE IN THE mountains of British Columbia, on the 15th of November in 1885. The name of the place was Scottish, as were a good many of the men gathered at trackside. They watched as Donald Smith, who had yet to become Lord Stratchcona, drove an iron spike that finished the thing they had built—the Canadian Pacific Railway (CPR).

Most Americans are aware of the driving of their own golden spike in 1869 at Promontory, Utah, as one of the pivotal events in the nation's history. For Canada, though, the completion of the transcontinental railway was arguably the pivotal event. The spike that linked the eastern and western segments of the CPR riveted together the 18-year-old nation as well.

Not coincidentally, the completion of a railroad from the St. Lawrence Valley to the Pacific opened up one of the most scenic tourist routes in the world, one which today's travelers can still enjoy in comfort. The Canadian Pacific has

left: *The Rockies in Spring offer truly majestic sights.*

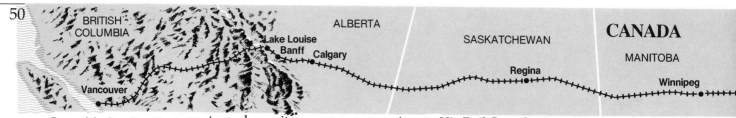

Route of the Canadian; Montreal to Vancouver, 3,045 miles.

turned over its passenger operations to Via Rail Canada, a government corporation that is roughly the equivalent of Amtrak in the United States. But the daily transcontinental Canadian remains on a par with the great long-distance trains, legends like Amtrak's Empire Builder and the Australian Railways' Indian Pacific.

The Canadian is not an adventure in extravagance like the restored Orient Express or South Africa's Blue Train, or even the Canadian Pacific limiteds of yore, which offered more choices in marmalade than today's trains have dinner entrees. Most of the rolling stock dates from the mid-fifties, the Indian summer of art deco streamlining: the lucite railings on the stairs between the lounge and the observation level actually light up at night. But the old cars are decently maintained, the beds in the sleeping compartments are comfortable, and linen still covers the dining tables. It all adds up to a pleasant, if not opulent, backdrop to the main attraction, which is nothing less than North America.

There is no better way than a 3,045-mile train trip to learn what this continent really looks like. Even if the clouds part, you can't get the picture from 30,000 feet; and as for driving, the sheer distances involved make the experience more of an endurance test than a revelation. No, the train is the way, and as fond as this traveler is of the change-at-Chicago American routes, the Canadian is the one that makes you feel as if you're swallowing North America whole.

The question of whether it works better from east-to-west or west-to-east might seem answerable only in terms of where you happen to be when you start out, but a case can be made for embarking from Montreal or Toronto (the train leaves every afternoon) and heading west. It all has to do with the way the topographical story unfolds and climaxes; the mountains are out west, and if you start in Vancouver you're watching the last act first.

The east-west run takes you through the suburbs of Toronto and the lake country of southern Ontario in darkness. When you slide open your window shade, you'll be in the vicinity of the much-maligned smelting town of Sudbury, but the slag heaps soon fade away and the immensity of the North Woods begins.

The North Woods—pines, birches, and a hundred-thousand lakes, serve as reminders that one-third of all the fresh water in the world is in Canada. The woods overlie the Canadian Shield, a vast belt of billion-year-old granite that alternately breaks the surface and dips below to saucer the treacherous muskeg

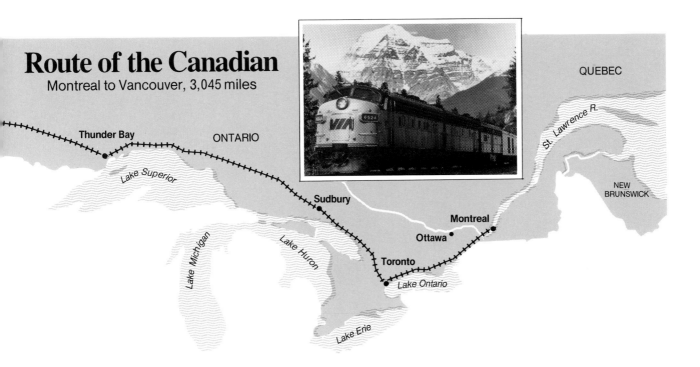

Route of the Canadian
Montreal to Vancouver, 3,045 miles

QUEBEC

Thunder Bay   ONTARIO

Lake Superior

St. Lawrence R.

NEW
BRUNSWICK

Sudbury

Montreal

Ottawa

Lake Michigan   Lake Huron

Toronto

Lake Ontario

Lake Erie

bogs that swallowed countless carloads of fill while the railway was being built.

By evening you are skirting the northern shores of Lake Superior. Here the roadbed, clawed from the face of the rock, hugs the bank with so little room to spare that the left-hand windows of the train might as well be the portholes of a ship.

Morning of the third day dawns with the Canadian barely emerging from the forest, and from the province of Ontario. But within a few miles the trees thin to sparseness, and the prairies begin almost precisely at the Manitoba border.

If the North Woods seemed endless, the prairies will prove to be their equal. You may want to get off the train for a day or two in Winnipeg, a likable, casual yet cosmopolitan city that invariably surprises first-time visitors with its cultural resources, art and historical museums, and restaurants reflecting the city's polyglot ethnic mix.

Take a good look at the Winnipeg skyline as the Canadian pulls out of the station. It's the loftiest thing you'll see for the next 850 miles, until the glass towers of Calgary loom into view. In between lie the wheatfields of Manitoba, Saskatchewan, and eastern Alberta, punctuated only by Regina (Saskatchewan's capital), a handful of prairie towns, and the ubiquitous, colorful wooden grain elevators. Out here, the sky is far bigger than anything beneath it.

For all the prairie's subtle grandeur, it begins to wear out its welcome by the morning of the fourth day. That is when you arrive in Calgary, an oil city like its cousins Denver and Dallas to the south. As in those other boomtowns, Calgary has turned its petrochemical pretensions into extravagant downtown architecture. If you can, take a day off here just to visit the Glenbow Museum, Canada's finest institution devoted to western art, ethnology, and social history.

No sooner do you leave Calgary—with the Canadian's windows scrubbed clean—than the tracks follow the Bow River into the foothills of the Rockies.

For the next eight hours, the Canadian becomes the greatest train in the world, simply by virtue of the route painstakingly carved through the mountains by the engineers and heroic work crews of a hundred years ago. To them, the terrain was a barely surmountable challenge, but it wasn't long before the railroad management saw the potential for tourism and built the sumptuous resort hotels at Banff and Lake Louise.

To this day it doesn't seem quite right to approach the Banff Springs or the Château Lake Louise except by train; one almost feels inclined to travel with a steamer trunk in the baggage car.

In winter, Banff and Lake Louise are where the skiers get off. It may seem unusual in this day and age to travel to a destination by long-distance train, but why not? Banff lies in the valley below Mt. Norquay and Sunshine Village, two top-notch areas. At Lake Louise there is Skiing Louise, Canada's largest ski complex, with 36 designated runs and eight lifts arrayed over three mountain faces. Shuttle buses connect the three areas with the Canadian Pacific and other hotels at Banff and Lake Louise.

Canada's North Woods is home to grazing deer.

You've come this far, so head for the coast

After cresting the Rockies and the adjacent Selkirk range, the Canadian begins its nighttime descent into the valleys of the turbulent Thompson and Fraser Rivers, through gorges charmingly named "Jaws of Death" and "Hell's Gate," and the Fraser Canyon itself. By daybreak the Fraser is broad and flat, approaching its finish at Vancouver, as is the 3,045-mile run of the Canadian.

In the three-and-one-half days and four nights since leaving Montreal, its passengers will have seen that Canada, though far vaster than Gaul, is divided into three parts—forest, prairies, and mountains. And they will have learned that those top-hatted Scots who met at Craigellachie just a century ago indeed had something to celebrate.

IF YOU GO

For more information, call Via Rail Canada at (800) 561-3949 or call a travel agent.

53

Father and daughter share magnificent mountain vistas.

Marion Laffey Fox

A RIDE ON THE MODERN-DAY ORIENT EXPRESS RECALLS AN ERA OF OPULENCE

A JOURNEY ON THE VENICE SIMPLON-ORIENT EXPRESS IS AN ELEGANT example of once-upon-a-time travel. With gourmet food, fresh flowers, and tinkling piano music, the trappings of yesterday are stunningly restored.

Once again this delightful train carries passengers almost the entire length of Europe. American entrepreneur James B. Sherwood rescued the train, haggling at auctions and spending five years on costly restorations before returning it to the rails in 1983.

In the fall of 1985, a dramatic Alpine route that passes through Swiss valleys and mountains and picturesque Austrian villages and crosses the Brenner Pass was added to the regular Italian run. This proved so successful that it has become the permanent route to Venice, with skier stops in Zurich, Landquart, and Chur in Switzerland, and Innsbruck and St. Anton in Austria.

On May 3, 1986, the Venice Simplon-Orient Express inaugurated service to Istanbul, augmenting its 32-hour sentimental journey from London to Venice. (This train is not to be confused with the Orient Express, operated by Society Expeditions, which offers rail tours using similarly restored cars.)

Weekly service will include a transfer from the train station in Venice to the refurbished Baltic ferry *Silja Star*, renamed *M.V. Orient Express*. Featuring the

left: *Boarding the Orient Express in London.*

only regularly scheduled service from Venice through the Corinthian Canal, the 835-passenger vessel offers a choice of accommodations ranging from super-deluxe suites with verandas and deluxe cabins to more modest quarters.

Although passengers may disembark in Istanbul, the eastward leg of the journey is not a simple ferry crossing to Turkey. It is really a week-long cruise that incorporates a stop in Istanbul with other calls at the island of Patmos, the ports of Piraeus and Katakolon, Greece, and Kusadasi, Turkey.

But a trip on the Venice Simplon-Orient Express needn't take days or even a week. If personal scheduling places you in Paris, Zurich, Innsbruck, or small places in between, you may want to avoid driving on unfamiliar roads or hurrying for planes, and take one leg of the scheduled trip on this train.

If you begin your journey in London's bustling Victoria Station, it's clear from the moment you arrive that this is no ordinary trip by train. Inside the main entrance, passengers are greeted with a modest but welcoming sign: "Board Here—Orient Express."

Beyond the sign, along the tracks leading to the special check-in point, the crowd turns amazingly homogeneous. Everyone is smiling. Women in designer suits escorted by men in marvelous tweeds stroll along carrying fine hand

Two stewards awaiting the passengers and porters in Venice.

luggage, hatboxes, and even bouquets of flowers, from nosegays of posies to a single rose. There is a sense of expectation in the air.

At the check-in desk, midway down the tracks, brown-uniformed aides assist with table and compartment assignments and baggage ticketing. They advise stowing most luggage in the baggage car and taking no more than one overnight case and a soft hanging bag into the small passenger compartments.

During check-in (passengers are advised to arrive almost two hours before departure), the elegant brown-and-cream-colored Pullman train rolls into the station, virtually noiselessly. Its appearance signals such excitement that a photographing frenzy ensues even before it comes to a complete stop.

Thus, the beginning of the journey is recorded in pictures showing travelers in front of signs, posters, and the gleaming crests on each individually named car.

On the first leg of the trip, which follows the Folkestone route to the English Channel, the train is very different from the one passengers will encounter in France, since it is made up largely of restaurant carriages with historic names.

Ours, called Cygnus, is a beautifully polished, handsomely restored time capsule with contrasting veneer designs, art deco mirrors, and brass-fitted overhead racks. Approximately 10 tables with window views are set with snowy cloth napkins, crystal, cutlery, and red carnations. Banquettes fill the ends of the car.

Serving luncheon in the sumptuous dining car.

After coats and bags have been whisked away, we settle into commodious, flocked-velvet armchairs. The city of London is left behind for rows of working-class cottages. Small farms fan out around tile-roofed villages. Meanwhile, at our table, crusty French bread is passed around, followed by a delightful cold duck paté with orange sauce and a rainbow of fresh vegetables.

An artistic garden salad seems the appropriate accompaniment for the lushness of Kent. Broad expanses of new winter wheat are contained by stone walls and neat hedgerows. Miles of orchards, bent with yellow, crimson, and green apples and ripening pears and plums, bake in the afternoon sun as we slip along the tracks.

It is all so civilized. So perfectly orchestrated. Dessert, a special confection of hardened milk chocolate filled with mocha soufflé, arrives just as the plains begin to yield to rounded hills. The half hour trip passes much too quickly and some passengers appear disgruntled at having to leave their cozy cocoons. But debarkation, customs check, and transfer to the Channel ferry is smoothly efficient.

Red carpets extend from the train to the gangplank. Once on board, passengers are directed to a special lounge outfitted with wide reclining seats and offering nonstop refreshment service. It feels and looks like an airplane pretending to be a train.

But it is *the* train, the *real* Orient Express, the half-mile of gleaming blue and gold cars, that everyone is straining to glimpse as we traipse through the welcoming area of Boulogne station three hours later. Here, another photographic session erupts as well-dressed grown-ups act like cavorting children.

Inside sleeping, dining, and lounge cars, ash and rosewood marquetry and veneer gleam from perfectly articulated art deco and art nouveau designs.

Each car differs in age, origin, and interior theme. Some feature popular motifs like tiger lilies, delicate baskets of flowers, fragile leaves, or dancing nymphs. Others are enhanced with black lacquer animals, mother-of-pearl inlay, or Lalique glass. All are outfitted with heavy pewter and polished brass.

Once passengers are escorted to their compartments, baggage is stowed, the whistle sounds, and the train whirs away. Tea is served almost immediately, and everyone unpacks finery for the evening.

Dusk unsuccessfully attempts to settle over the gentle Normandy countryside. One by one, rose-shaded lamps are lit in each compartment. There is nothing visible in the pastoral silence now, except an isolated glow of a farmhouse or the brief flash of a town.

Passengers drift in

Dinner is served at 6:30, 9, or 10:30 p.m. Happily, we are able to book the 9 o'clock seating, which allows plenty of time for dressing as well as a leisurely hour to mix with other guests and listen to piano tunes in one of the elaborate lounge cars.

This is even more fun than anticipated, as passengers drift in, attired in

The Swiss countryside offers spectacular vistas.

everything from sequined flapper dresses, tiaras, vintage capes, and veiled hats to contemporary evening wear. By the time dinner is announced, the flower-filled car resembles a festive Agatha Christie stage set, creating a mood that prevailed for the rest of the journey.

We were dining on poached salmon, filet mignon garnished with tiny vegetables, a selection of cheeses, and dessert, during the stop in Paris. By the time we were on our way again, the rocking of the train was creating its own lullaby.

Upper and lower berths, swaddled in ironed linen, transform each small compartment into irresistible nests. (Each roomette also contains a tiny bureau with flip-top sink for shaving and teeth brushing. Other facilities, located at both ends of each car, make robe and slippers absolute necessities.)

In the morning, many of us are up at 7 o'clock, in time to inspect Zurich station and lean out the windows (they all open) to greet the awakening Alps.

After breakfast, compartments revert back to velvet-couched sitting rooms. But their cozy comfort is largely ignored as passengers prowl the passageways or sit transfixed before windows, watching the spectacular scenery. At one moment the train teeters on the banks of pure mirror lakes; the next, it follows pebbly streams. We return shy greetings of waving blond children who call out as we pass.

Six miles from Innsbruck another engine called a "crocodile" is attached to the train. Now one will push and the other will pull us over the towering mountain valleys and passes, the most daring part of the trip. At times, it's possible to see the entire length of the train, spanning a curve or inching up steep inclines. Onion-domed churches and geranium-laden chalets become specks in the distance. "It's getting pretty dramatic, isn't it?" an anxious-looking woman asks her husband, just before we pierce the dampness of the Arlberg Tunnel.

On the other side, there is a crispness in the air. It has a bite, scented with wood-burning stoves and fresh, thick stands of spruce.

Walled, medieval villages

The Brenner Pass with its splendid bridges is eventually followed by walled medieval villages and ocher-colored stone hamlets. Brooding above and beyond, the crevices of the Dolomites preside over this self-contained land, with miles of unyielding stone faces that finally soften into waves of ripening vines.

Lunch, another formal affair, is followed by afternoon tea. Again the sun dips low, then vanishes, this time into a misty Italian dusk.

"Ah, I hate to leave," an English gentleman sighs as we disembark in Venice. "This journey reminds me of the grand days of travel, when we didn't rush to the airport to continue our rush from point A to point B. Yes, I must do this again and continue to Istanbul."

It was impossible not to agree.

N. Lofthouse

THE NIGHT TRAIN TO VICTORIA FALLS

IT'S A HOT NIGHT. FIREFLIES GLOW IN THE GRASS BESIDE THE TRACKS. Up ahead, the big steam engine pounds down through the low veld toward the Zambezi River. I lean on the our coach's window ledge and watch the shadowy round huts of an Africa kraal go by in the darkness.

For someone as irresistibly drawn to trains as I am, this is rail travel at its finest—steam in its full glory. This is the night train to the Victoria Falls.

The falls, in south-central Africa on the border between Zimbabwe and Zambia, has attracted visitors from all over the world for more than 100 years, ever since David Livingstone first visited here in 1855.

Most people today arrive by plane, since the air service from larger African cities is good. But for those who wish to see something of the countryside of south-ern Africa and get close to its people, I recommend the night train from Bula-wayo—with a few caveats: This is not a gleaming, high-speed train but an African train that runs on "African time," with stops at all hours for coal and water, passing freights, ash-pan cleaning, and engine exchanges. The air conditioning is by means of windows lowered on leather straps— which let in the breeze but also

The Bulawayo locomotive.

following pages: *One way to get there is by steam engine— chugging across the grasslands of Africa.*

left: *Aerial view of the wonder of Victoria Falls.*

Zimbabwe, highlighting Victoria Falls and the Harare-Livingstone railroad.

black coal dust. Toilet paper is usually missing from the lavatories; so you'll want to carry your own. And the tiny buffet car, which doubles as a stand-up bar, is usually crowded and noisy.

But these are minor inconveniences, compared with the singularity of the occasion. After all, how often does one get a chance to ride across the grasslands of Africa, en route to one of the world's great natural wonders, under a sky brilliant with stars, behind one of the giants of the all-but-extinct era of steam travel?

Bulawayo, where the train originates, is Zimbabwe's second-largest city, 275 miles southeast of Victoria Falls. The train has 19 passenger coaches, with economy class up front (very crowded, not recommended for tourist travel); standard or first-class sleeping coaches at the rear (clean, comfortable, and comparatively private, with two- or four-berth units); and the buffet car in the middle, which, despite the crowded conditions, serves hot, well-prepared meals.

Each evening at 7, the big Manchester-built Garratt engine leaves the Bulawayo steam shed and heads out into the countryside, northwest, toward the Zambezi River.

The 12-hour journey is a lively one, filled with the color and sounds of Africa on the move—women going to market or to show off new babies, men returning to the communal lands from work in the cities, children off to visit cousins or married sisters.

Outside Bulawayo, the villages bunch up one after another like knots on a string—Mpopoma, Luveve, Nyamandhlovu, Umzibani. As each one emerges from the darkness, the train slows to a stop. Doors bang open. People come and go in a tangle of bright cloth and babies and plastic bags.

There is an outburst of frenzy as the conductor moves nimbly through the coaches to make sure no one gets on without paying.

Then, silence. The whistle blows, the cylinders hiss steam, the connecting rods clank, and once again we move off into the darkness.

By midnight the train has moved into the open countryside, and we settle down to a lulling pattern of clank and sway, chuff and groan. I climb into my bunk and drift off to sleep, waking every now and then to check our progress. Outside, the night is bathed in moonlight. A herd of impala watches silently as we pass by.

Next morning, a few hours late because of a poorly steaming engine, we arrive at a little bougainvillea-covered railway station in the heart of the town of Victoria Falls and a few steps from the historic Victoria Falls Hotel.

Even travelers not staying at this hotel usually like to take a moment to look it over. It was constructed in 1905 as a bunkhouse for railway workers building the bridge across the gorge between Zimbabwe and Zambia (then known as Southern and Northern Rhodesia). Since then, the hotel has become one of

Africa's most elegant resorts, the kind of place with spacious sitting rooms, thick carpets, and white-jacketed waiters bearing silver tea trays down quiet corridors.

On its rambling terrace, you can sip a cool drink and watch the trains passing over the 657-foot-long railway bridge and, beyond that, the spray rising from the falls.

Cecil Rhodes, the Cape Colony industrialist who spearheaded much of the development of the two Rhodesias at the turn of the century, decreed that the bridge should be located so as to catch the spray from the falls as the coaches passed over it. It was a grandly romantic idea very typical of Rhodes. His style was always theatrical, and his vision of a Cape-to-Cairo railway was one of the consuming passions of his life.

Below the hotel, a trail leads down through the woods to the great waterfall itself. The affect that Victoria Falls has on people, particularly first-time visitors, is compelling. More than a mile wide, 355 feet high, and with an average flow of 38,000 cubic feet of water per second, it is awesome in its power and savage beauty.

It is also strangely ethereal, because of its mists and elusive rainbows. People often become so absorbed in their contemplation of the falls that they stand transfixed at the cliff edge, unmindful of the heat, the humidity, the drenching spray, and one another.

So it was with David Livingstone. On Nov. 16, 1855, the explorer-missionary beached his canoe on an island on the upper edge of the falls and peered below. He was so moved by what he saw that he wrote in his journal "scenes so lovely must have been gazed upon by angels in their flight."

There is a bronze statue of Livingstone in the Victoria Falls National Park. It is a massive, stolid, grim-faced likeness, standing in a small clearing at the edge of the falls. It commands what surely must be one of the most magnificent views in the area, all down the length of the wide chasm from Devil's Cataract to Danger Point. Most people begin their walking tour of the falls from this point, and the brooding presence of Livingstone lends a sense of history and solemnity to the occasion.

Since the magnitude of the falls can be best appreciated from the air, however, consider taking United Air's "Flight of the Angels" tour. The flight offers a superb view of the Zambezi as it glides over the lip of the falls and thunders down into the chasm, sending plumes of spray so high that they can be seen from 20 miles away.

From the air, you get an understanding of how the waterfall has worked itself back upriver over successive geological ages, creating an accordion-pleat effect of deep folds in the landscape. The 15-minute trip costs about $25 per person and is well worth the money.

IF YOU GO

Write Zimbabwe National Railways, P.O. Box 596, Bulawayo, Zimbabwe, East Africa, for information on train schedules and rates. The Bulawayo and District Publicity Association (P.O. Box 861, Bulawayo) is an excellent source of information on hotels and other tourist attractions nearby. For information in the United States, write to the Embassy of Zimbabwe, 2852 McFill Terrace, N.W., Washington, D.C. 20008; or call (202) 332-7100. Or contact the Zimbabwe Tourist Office, New York, N.Y. 10020, (212) 307-6565. In Canada, contact the High Commission of the Republic of Zimbabwe, 112 Kent St., Suite 1315, Place de Ville, Tower B, Ottawa, Ontario K1P 5P7 Canada; (613) 237-4388.

Elsa Ditmars

A RAIL PASS PUTS EUROPE AT YOUR FEET

TRAIN BUFFS ENJOYING THE SCENERY FROM COZY COMPARTMENTS
are pretty smug about their freedom from traffic and tour guides, from blizzardy
or blistering weather.

Indeed we are.

But now I've latched onto a further advantage in train travel: the extraordi-
narily versatile, small, plastic-covered rail pass. It is a true blank check for
travelers in Europe who get their kicks dismantling an itinerary.

The ferry across the English Channel to Dover was delayed, giving me an
extra 30 minutes in France. I stood on the Calais pier and let my imagination spin
like a wheel with heady possibilities, but my thoughts kept returning to those
creamy-soft, little-heeled Florentine pumps I had seen earlier on my trip.

Four days remained on my two-month Eurailpass. Why not? I grabbed my
suitcase, dashed to Quai 3 and, with barely a skipped beat, was on my way back
to Florence.

With the jubilation of a kid playing hooky on the first spring day, I collapsed
into the compartment seat just as the train pulled out heading south. Chalk one
up for solo travel, the freedom to bounce around on whim.

It was 3:45. I checked my Thomas Cook's Continental Timetable and found
I was on an express to Rome, with stops at Basel, Milan, and Florence. Once again

*Streaking through the French
countryside.*

left: *Viewing Venice by gondola
through the maze of canals.*

It's not uncommon to find an artist sketching the timeless Venetian waterscapes.

I was struck by the marvelous flexibility we rail-pass holders enjoy compared to other travelers. I would not have considered driving a rented car 1,000 miles down to Italy and 1,000 miles back for a pair of shoes, no matter how lovingly handcrafted. And air fare would have doubled the already steep price tag on that pair of shoes.

When the conductor slid open the compartment door, I bought a berth to Florence and changed cars. An extravagance, yes, but worth every centime, and it came with a complimentary breakfast in bed.

At 10:35 the morning sun sparkled on the Arno, and I made a beeline to the small shop on Via Tornabuoni, a tree-lined avenue of Renaissance palaces, fine stores, and offices, widely proclaimed to be "one of the noblest, most perfect streets in the world."

Settled on a pale green, velvet sofa, with my floppy handbag draped over a tiny gilt-rimmed end table, I asked for the *scarpina marroné*, size 37.

The ambience of this shoe salon makes the most exclusive Rodeo Drive bootery in Beverly Hills seem garish by comparison. On display were fewer than 10 shoes. But there was no trace of snobbery in the *maggiordomo*. He smiled a touch wistfully and dispatched an assistant to a nearby dress shop. In a few minutes she returned carrying a beige wool skirt. I could sense their pain at contemplating the lovely shoes below the cuffs of my faded Italian jeans.

With the borrowed skirt—Ah. *Va benissima!*

I held them gently in my hands, those sweet little tailored caramel pumps. For such perfection $110 did not seem out of line.

On an elegance chart I put Florence at the top, for here even the tourists appear to dress with more respect for the formally attired Florentines.

At last, properly shod and wool-skirted, I revisited my favorite places— polished little heels clicking brightly on the marble floors of the Palazzo Vecchio, up the stone steps of the Bargello, echoing along the vast central aisle of the Dominican church of Santa Maria Novella.

Now, caught up in the fun of revisiting favorite places, I decided to catch the overnight to Munich at 8 o'clock.

The train was too crowded and noisy. After an hour I got off at Bologna and caught a sleeper to Vienna instead. More cheers for ad-lib traveling.

Sleepers offer a variety of accommodations, from inexpensive couchettes (facing triple-decker berths, mere shelves with blanket and pillow), to single bed-rooms with wash basin, towels, soap, a carafe of drinking water, and a lock on the door. For exclusive use in a single or double bedroom the supplemental fare is about equal to a first-class hotel room.

The train arrived promptly at 9:10, giving me a whole day in Austria's dazzling capital.

IF YOU GO

For more information write to Eurailpass, P.O. Box 325, Old Greenwich, CT 06870-0325, or contact a travel agent.

It was Sunday; I had just time to taxi to the Hofburgkapelle to hear the Vienna Boys' Choir. They sing at early service every Sunday from mid-September to late June, but I'd always missed them. My new shoes glowed prettily in the candlelit chapel.

After church I decided to lunch in the rotating café-restaurant atop the 826-foot observation tower in Danube Park. A clear day, a magnificent view of Vienna.

The day was topped off with a recital at Musikerein, home of the Vienna Philharmonic, before catching the 11 o'clock to well, why not? Venice.

One special souvenir I'm bringing back from this adventure-by-rail is a statuette of the Roman god Mercury, about the size of a Hollywood Oscar. His feet in winged sandals are no more buoyant and poised for flight than are mine in my 2000-mile, three-city calfskin pumps.

On the Vienna-Venice express I had a couchette compartment all to myself. You'd seldom get a break like that during peak season. In fact, summer travelers often reserve seats or berths on the international trains before leaving home.

For my extra day in Venice, the new shoes were carefully stowed in my duffel while I slogged around in the cold drizzle in my dependable, old Wellington boots.

Happiness turned out to be that impromptu return to three cities I'd loved most during the planned part of my trip. A textbook example of serendipity. A plus on the solo travel scorecard.

One help on my quick trip was Thomas Cook's Continental Timetable, published 12 times a year, priced at $19.95 each in the United States. It requires a large coat pocket, but I was endlessly grateful for this travel aid.

Surprisingly useful for train travel is a radio or recorder with a headset. Once my compartment mate happened to be a stupefying nonstop talker. All I wanted was undisturbed contemplation of the Alpine scenery, so I offered him my headset plugged into the entire Beethoven Ninth, and gained for myself a full hour's grace.

It was a kick to run the tape of Schubert's "Wanderer's Fantasy" while strolling past the composer's statue in Stadtpark, and to switch to "Tales From the Vienna Woods" in a dark grove of pines—but not easy to keep my pretty shoes from waltzing away on the grass.

The French countryside by train is dotted with many a chateau.

Betty M. Ames

ON THE
TRACKS OF
MARCO POLO

MY TRAIN-BUFF HUSBAND WAS ECSTATIC ABOUT CHUGGING FROM London to Xian, China. I had a strong sense of trepidation, since I had braved the Red Arrow from Peking to London—via Mongolia, Siberia, and Moscow—only the year before.

But as the plans unfolded, I began to realize that this trip, initially offered three years ago by Voyages Jules Verne in London, was a real first in itinerary and mode of travel. Not only would my husband and I have a compartment to ourselves on this maiden voyage, but the entire train would be private with the exception of some of the European rail lines, and even then our tour would have private cars.

When we went, the trip was called "2100 Years of the Silk Road." Since then, it has been renamed "On the Tracks of Marco Polo." The send-off from London, we found, was indeed fitting for an incredible 45-day adventure of 7,011 miles.

At night we were booked into hotels that were the best each stop had to offer, and in the larger cities the accommodations were excellent. Sometimes a two-night stand gave us extra time for exploration, as well as the usually fine tours offered in each city. Lavish meals were prepared for us in every country, either on the train or in restaurants.

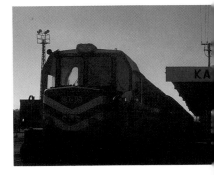

Kars is the last stop in Turkey before crossing the border into the Soviet Union.

left: *The world's second largest wooden church can be found in Alma-Ata, Kazakhstan.*

Dracula's many-tiered castle, high on a hill.
right: *The eleventh century churches of Cappadocia in the Goreme Valley were all carved out of volcanic rock.*

After boarding our train in London, we visited Paris, Salzburg, and Vienna. In Budapest, our hotel, the luxurious Intercontinental, overlooked the Danube, and on the train to Bucharest we followed the Danube and looked out on red-tiled roofs and green hills.

I would have thought the trip by steam train from Bucharest to Sinaia in Transylvania, up an autumn-colored valley beside a rushing river, was the most beautiful, if we had not bused through even more magnificent countryside to see Dracula's many-tiered castle, high on a hill. Yes, Dracula lived there from 1456 to 1462. He was a hero as a fighter against Turks. "Vlad the Impaler," he was called, but he was not a vampire, as English novelist Bram Stoker would have him.

The first part of our journey followed the route of the original Orient Express trains. At Varna, Bulgaria, we boarded ships, just as the Orient Express travelers used to do, and slept overnight as we crossed the Black Sea. We awakened as the ship passed through the Bosporus and into the minareted splendor of Istanbul. Some travelers left us at this point, but 100 of us began the Silk Road across Turkey by steam train. We were intrigued by views of mud huts and barren mountains.

As we moved eastward in Turkey, the hotels, had they been star-ranked, would have dropped stars rapidly as we progressed. Lodgings were in small towns, with few visitors from the West.

We felt so engulfed in a culture very different from our own that every new experience called for tolerance and brought the excitement of discovery. To have our own room with bath seemed remarkable to us. From our hotel balcony in Erzincan, Turkey, we overlooked the only paved street, saw people hauling water from the town pump, and women covered in brown burlap with only their eyes showing.

From an overnight in Kayseri, in the province of Cappadocia, we bused to the Goreme Valley, where we had the thrill of seeing churches and homes dating from the 11th century carved right into wind-shaped columns of volcanic rock. The churches came complete with carved pillars and religious frescoes painted on the cave walls.

After six days we came to the border between Turkey and the Soviet Union. It was an exciting and somewhat tense moment as we left our Turkish train, crossed a platform, and boarded brand-new sleeping cars on the Soviet train. It had come across the 100-yard barrier, closed for 35 years, for the express purpose of taking us aboard.

Our train took us through the republics of Georgia, Azerbaijan, Uzbekistan, and Kazakhstan. Beautiful, mountainous Tbilisi, the Caspian Sea, and the markets of Bukhara highlighted our journey.

At fabled Samarkand, where my husband and I went off on our own to the Pamirs with a hired driver, we had an exhilarating hike and met two villagers

74

who had come by donkey to fill baskets with wild apples for market. Later, we came upon a small girl and her little brother tending a large herd of sheep.

Final stops in the Soviet Union were modern Tashkent, where 40 percent of the city was rebuilt after a 1966 earthquake, and Alma-Ata, snuggled at the foot of the towering Ala Tau Mountains, where the Medeo Olympic Speed Skating Rink was built at an altitude of 5,000 feet. Then our hosts bused us to the Chinese border 185 miles away.

Traveling through a vast desert with snowy mountains in the distance, we rounded a bend into the Charyn River Canyon and stopped. There, in the middle of nowhere, we found tables laid out for us, and waiters barbecuing shish kebab and serving tea.

The next surprise came a few hours later. When we drove into the isolated town of Panfilov, a great portion of the 30,000 residents were standing on the street corners to welcome us and gaze on their first tourists. A sumptuous banquet with all the town dignitaries was spread out in the town hall, and local musicians and dancers entertained nonstop. The facial features of the people reflected the fact that we were nearing China.

We felt an air of suspense when at nightfall we reached the barbed-wire border that had not been open to tourists since 1949. Customs accomplished, we were delivered by the Soviet bus to the border. We disembarked, waved goodbye to our Soviet guides, and walked to the Chinese buses. We drove a short distance to a great hoopla of percussion and dancers.

From the old city of Inning, where we spent the night, we went by bus over the Tianshan Mountains. At 8,000 feet, the sapphire blue of Lake Sayram suddenly spread out before us. As we traveled beside it, a herd of wild horses galloped by in the desert.

We saw camels and yerts, and farmers driving their trucks at break-neck speed to bring their produce to market. After an overnight in a guesthouse in the small, dusty town of Shihezi, we arrived at Urumchi, the Western Province's biggest city, and checked into a large, modern hotel.

Two days later we boarded our smooth Chinese steam train and settled into our lace-curtained compartment that we had for the rest of the trip. Our train waited for us while we spent nights at comfortable hotels in Turfan, Dunhuang, Jiuquan, and Lanzhou, then chugged through the spectacular Wei River Valley with its mountains, terraced for farming on even the steepest slopes.

The last stop, Xian, provided the warmest welcome of all. Five hundred railway workers' children in costume and makeup greeted us on the platform, rhythmically waving pompoms, beating drums, and saying "warm welcome" in Chinese. Our stay in Xian was the end of our magical voyage, where the world's wonders flashed before us as though by the touch of a wand.

Vacations that Test
the Skills

Biking Downhill
from Hawaii's Haleakala

A Jogger's Guide
to World Travel

Atop the Grand Teton

Great Barrier Reef

Hiker's Paradise

John Edward Young

BIKING DOWNHILL FROM HAWAII'S HALEAKALA

THE GOOD NEWS IS THAT IT'S A BIKE RIDE. THE BAD NEWS IS THAT IT'S 38.2 miles long. The great news is that it's all downhill. The worst news is that you have to get up at about 2 a.m.

The best news of all is that it's worth it!

Mt. Haleakala, the "House of the Sun," is a broad, brooding dormant volcano rising 10,023 feet above the sea and dominating Maui, the second largest of the Hawaiian Islands chain.

The view from the summit on a clear day and at sunset is spectacular. But the best view, we were assured as we staggered sleepy-eyed aboard the minibus that was to carry us to the top, was at sunrise. A sight that moved Mark Twain to exclaim, "It is the sublimest spectacle I ever witnessed."

It was from the summit of this largest dormant volcano in the world that our bike ride was to begin.

Eleven of us sat in the bus, jostling along as our cheerful guide, Deedee Pachico, gave a nonstop narration of what we were driving past during the inky three-and-a-half-hour drive above the clouds.

"Most of the vegetation we're passing has been imported," Deedee said as we swept past fields of sugar cane and pineapples. "Only above 7,000 feet are the plants indigenous, including the rare silversword. I know it's too dark to see

left: *Dawn at Haleakala, Maui.*

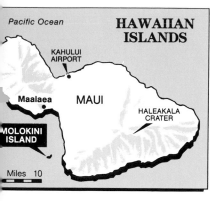

Maui is one of the six largest islands in the active volcanic Hawaiian chain.

anything, but you'll get to see it all on the way down."

At the summit we jumped off the bus and promptly jumped back on board. Somehow you don't expect to freeze on Maui, even at this altitude, but the temperature had dropped to 34 degrees, and the wind whirled around, adding to the chill.

Hooded yellow nylon windbreakers, baggy matching pants, and black helmets made us look like a bunch of extras from the set of *Star Trek IV*, but they helped stave off the biting cold. With the planet Venus as our major light source, we edged slowly and carefully to the rim of Haleakala, as sheets of tiny silvery ice crystals crackled under foot.

Here we waited patiently for the mythical demigod Maui's promise to be fulfilled. It was Maui, according to legend, who snared the sun in its journey across the sky and held it until it promised to travel more slowly over these verdant Pacific isles.

Dawn finally arrived wondrously as the sun broke with a flash across the blanket of clouds, lining them with a thin edge of gold. In a few minutes the mouth of this great volcano lit up before us—a crater so vast that it could swallow Manhattan Island!

Soon the light turned the sky to soft hues of golden pink and revealed a desolate, lunar landscape. If not the "sublimest spectacle" we had ever witnessed, it did bring a few more goose bumps to our arms.

Anyway, there was no time to linger and wax poetic. Back at the parking lot, our bikes were waiting, and the long black asphalt road stretched like a ribbon before us.

"OK, gang! Grab a bike and take a practice spin around the parking lot, and let's go. We've got a three-hour ride ahead of us," Deedee shouted above the howling wind.

I picked out a Diamondback Sand Streaker bike with cantilever brake system.

We went over the rules of the road: Don't pass anyone, don't look around, stay 25 feet apart, no freewheeling, stay to the right, etc.

"If you break the rules or if you can't keep up, it's back in the bus," Deedee warned.

And down we went, slowly at first, from the frosty, barren peaks through more temperate grassy cattle country, around hairpin turns, and stopping for an occasional picture. Great stands of eucalyptus trees along the road gave off the heady smell of spice as we passed beneath them.

Deedee, always in control, was in constant telecommunication with our bus driver, who followed watchfully. If anyone fell out of line, Deedee was quickly informed.

At 10 miles we made a pit stop at a visitor center. There we got a close look at the silversword plants and nene geese. The silverswords, once common here, are now rare and protected. Not many years ago it was considered great sport to uproot them and roll them down the mountain. It was little known then that it takes seven to thirty years for a single plant to mature, bloom, and die. Only then does it cast off its seeds.

Unfortunately, cattle, sheep, and feral goats and pigs brought in by early settlers acquired a taste for the young plants.

Nene geese, Hawaii's national bird, haven't fared any better. They have been moved to this higher, protected area to save them from extinction. As part of the process of adapting, they have begun to develop short claws on their webbed feet to help them climb the rough terrain.

Back on our bikes, we continued our descent with greater speed and confidence.

"There are 29 180-degree turns in the next 13 miles," said Deedee. "It's called 'Bikers' Paradise.' Let's go!" (You'll find everything good on these islands referred to as "paradise.")

We zipped through the zigzag turns and finished the trip through flat fields of sugar cane and pineapples in fine fettle.

A breakfast of eggs Benedict, French toast, or fritatta was laid out and waiting in the little town of Makawao.

"I did it! I did it!" one older woman from Michigan exclaimed as she pulled off her helmet. "Now I have something to tell the girls at bridge!"

"It was like traveling through three different countries: arctic, temperate, and tropical," said one of the male members of the party.

"I loved the smells and the scenery," said another, and she added, "I'd like to back up and do it all over again."

IF YOU GO

Three companies offer bike rides down Mt. Haleakala. Each charges about $75, including a pickup at your hotel. Continental breakfast and lunch are also included.

The companies are listed in the free brochures available at hotels, condominiums, and rental car agencies on the island.

Later morning and afternoon trips are available daily. All excursions are limited to around 14 people, so book early.

Dress warmly. A heavy sweater or light jacket is a good idea. The windbreakers that are provided aren't enough. As you descend, clothes may be shed.

Binoculars and sun glasses are not essential, but you might find them worth carrying.

A close view of the Haleakala crater reveals the desolate lunar landscape.

Peter I. Rose

A JOGGER'S GUIDE TO WORLD TRAVEL

FOR ME THERE IS NOTHING BETTER THAN GETTING UP AT THE CRACK of dawn, slipping out of the hotel in the middle of a strange city, making a snap decision about whether to turn left or right, and then jogging off on a new adventure. I do it all the time, in the States and abroad.

Over the past 10 years I have run around the Ringstrasse in Vienna, down dusty roads in suburban Nairobi, through back alleys in Hong Kong, in and out of little villages high above Bellagio, along bustling avenues in Peking, and along the banks of the Liffey, the Thames, the Seine, the Rhine, and many other rivers.

Such running around the world has a special quality to it. It is a kind of inversion of the oxymoron "same difference," which we used to say as kids. The *different sameness* of what I do to keep in shape *and* to see new places before starting a day's work is a most satisfying fringe benefit of my itinerant life-style. Research projects, meetings, and lectures keep me on the move.

While I have occasion to meet many people and to visit many interesting places on my trips, it is on early-morning jogs and off-hour weekend wanderings that I can especially feel the wondrous unity and amazing diversity of the family of man. Time and again I am struck by continuities and connections between me and those whose habitats provide me with "field sites" for comparative study.

left: *Under the shadow of Big Ben, runners in London clock miles and enjoy the sights.*

Pre-dawn Aspen "field site" gives a perfect route for watching the sunrise through the mountains.

It's when I am literally on the road that much of what I study and write about, namely, culture and character, becomes most personally meaningful.

Most of the people I've encountered in my off-the-tourist-route excursions are warm and friendly. In places unused to the likes of me, they are sometimes a bit confused by my half-dressed presence as I suddenly appear from around a cobblestoned corner or over the brow of a brick-laid hill. I have seen the proverbial double take as early risers look at me, stop, and look again, in cities such as Madrid; Mexico City; New Delhi; Dubrovnik, Yugoslavia; Suva in the Fijis; and Sendai, Japan. Then, usually, they smile.

Sometimes they do more. I was once stopped by an elderly street cleaner on a corner in the center of Graz, Austria. Shaking her finger, she lectured me in German for at least 10 minutes, explaining that "one must not cross the road against the light," even though it was 5:30 a.m. and there was no traffic in the area.

"Rules," she said, "are rules. And here, in Austria, they are obeyed."

Not, apparently, in Italy. There, by contrast, on numerous occasions I have been laughed at by passersby as I *waited* for a light to change in the first rush of traffic of the day.

Like a Pied Piper, I've been followed by groups of Chinese children along Shanghai's Bund and down by the beach at Penang, Malaysia. I've been cheered by Swedes who called "Hup, hup, hup" as I ran along Stockholm's quay and by New Zealanders as I headed into the hills above Christchurch.

My obsession has rarely gotten me into serious trouble. On the contrary, it has often opened doors. I've found that occasional stops to talk or to try to communicate with the local people can pay off in a variety of ways.

I remember a morning in Xian, China; I ran from the grounds of my big, Soviet-style hotel, off to the right, toward the center. There, in the giant plaza of the new provincial building, were hundreds of people in groups ranging from six or eight to forty or fifty, all doing their exercises.

Few paid much attention to me as I loped by, but I was most curious about them.

I ran for another mile or so, then retraced my route. As I returned to the area of activity, I stopped nearby and watched. At one point a young man came up to me and, in schoolbook English, said, "You jog, sir."

"Yes," I said.

"I do not jog; I exercise with this," he said, showing me his wooden sword.

I asked him to tell me what he did with it. He bade me to follow him, and we walked past several clusters of older people doing a kind of stylized shadow-boxing to a waiting group of four young men. My new friend nodded to me, then joined the others. They started an elaborate routine of thrusts and parries, all accompanied by routinized foot movements.

While participating in the swordplay, the young Chinese who brought me there did not look at me, but I did notice him smile when, after 10 minutes or so, I waved at him and took my leave.

There was also the time I was running in the woods near the Holmenkollen ski jump high above the city of Oslo. It was a fantastic fall morning. Everything was in tones of yellow, green, and blue.

Quite unexpectedly, I heard footsteps behind me. Someone was gaining on me. I suppressed the urge to speed up and decided to let him or her pass. He, who turned out to be a man about my age, didn't. He merely caught up, fell in with my pace, and started to chat.

We ran along together for another two miles or so, getting to know each other and to learn that, not only was he also a university professor, but one who was in my field and who would be attending my lecture that very afternoon.

The next morning I ran with him in another part of the city and in the afternoon he took me to a fishing village I would never have seen. That was 12 years ago. We are still in touch.

What advice can I give to fellow runners who are traveling?

First, if you want to take the tried and true routes, ask a concierge where you can run. It's pleasant to discover that, even in those places where the locals think joggers are a bit crazy, the activity has become sufficiently commonplace that they can usually tell you where to go.

Second, don't let your desire to get in the miles detract you from the fringe benefits. Watch where you put your feet, as you always must in strange places; but also slow your pace so you have time to look around, sniff the air, drink in the atmosphere.

Third, keep your shirt on. I have learned that even in warm weather ports, where runners are not uncommon, local customs demand a certain decorum, even in the wee hours when most of those who set the standards are still fast asleep.

All senses are alerted to drink in the atmosphere of a San Francisco Bay run.

Mark Ragan

ATOP
THE GRAND
TETON

GARY WAITE, A FARMER FROM MISSOURI, HANGS BY HIS FINGERTIPS from a narrow ledge 12,000 feet above sea level. He has a rope around his waist and an expert climber on the other end of the rope to stop him if he starts to fall.

Clutching the wall, Waite can see the sun splaying off the sea-green lakes in the valley below and a cluster of tents that now appear as splotches of yellow and red on the horizon.

He moves up the mountain slowly, slipping his hand over an outcropping of rock to reach a granite slab where instructor David Carman is waiting. He gulps down his reward—a granola bar and a few mouthfuls of a cold drink—and we take our positions to continue up this 13,770-foot mountain.

There are many ways to see western Wyoming's Tetons: from your car, from the airplanes that soar overhead on their way to Jackson Hole, or from the lodges in Grand Teton National Park. But some people choose to see them up close and, more important, to overcome them—to stand on top and know that it took something extraordinary, possibly even obsessive, to make it to the summit.

Climbing is not for just anyone who feels the allure of these craggy peaks. But for people in good condition who delight in overcoming obstacles and their own fears, climbing the Grand Teton can be the ultimate thrill, one that stays with you for a lifetime.

Mark Ragan resting along the route.

left: *David Carman setting up belay on the Grand.*

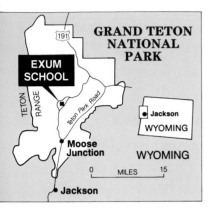

Grand Teton National Park, pinpointing Exum School, with inset of Wyoming, highlighting area of larger map.

Today Carman, a guide from the Exum Guide Service and School of American Mountaineering based at Jenny Lake in the park, is charged with escorting me and Waite, who is 38 years old and returning for his fourth ascent up the Grand Teton. A 20-year veteran of climbing, Carman is no stranger to the mountain, having completed the first winter ascent of its north ridge some years ago. This morning he decided to delay the climb until the sun can melt the snow from last night's storm on the mountain's southern face.

What makes these mountains so dramatic is that they rise so sharply, shooting up from the flat valley floor. Mountaineers from around the world come to try their skills on these famous peaks.

The physical demands on a climber are tough; it helps to train before attempting the climb. Still, Carman enjoys regaling his clients with stories of Harry, the 71-year-old former electrician from St. Louis who has scaled half a dozen Teton peaks with Carman in the lead.

Climbing the Grand Teton is the crowning accomplishment for most Exum graduates, coming usually after two days of practice on the rocks above Jenny Lake. The service's guides take nearly 300 climbers up the mountain every summer and instruct twice that many in daily rock-climbing classes on the boulders and low-sloping walls in the shadow of the Tetons.

But climbers also learn from the other climbers they meet on the mountain and at the base camp. Every Exum student spends the night before climbing the Grand Teton in the school's permanent hut at the base of the mountain. They usually share that camp with some of the guides.

The storm that blew over our camp the previous night forged a bond among the guides and their clients. As the lightning crashed outside, striking the nearby mountains, the veteran climbers swapped tales of climbing in Nepal and China. And they joked about the storm that rocked the vinyl hut throughout the night, dumping rain, hail, and then snow.

"Has anyone noticed the tent is glowing?" quipped Jack Tackle, as a lightning bolt found its mark not too far away. Tackle had just returned from a wintry attempt on Alaska's fierce Mount Hunter. He and another climber spent a month in a tent waiting for a snowstorm to subside.

The jokes then turned to climbing. Rick Black, a veteran Teton climber and venture capitalist who was returning to scale routes he first climbed 10 years ago, advised us: "You never talk bad about your partner when he's on the other side of the rope."

Next morning, the weather broke at 10 a.m. The sun appeared and began to warm the southern face of the mountain. Carman was still worried about slippery snow and ice on the mountain as we left the base to start our climb.

We made slow but steady progress. Carman took us up a moderately difficult route, because Waite and I both had some experience climbing. But the experience didn't take away the thrill—the awareness of being so high and of getting there yourself.

We were reminded of the dangers of mountain climbing the previous day as we hiked up the trail to the base camp. At Garnet Canyon, we met a shaken climber who had fallen and was limping past us to the trailhead below. He related the story of his slip down a patch of ice onto a field of boulders.

There are risks in climbing, but it all seemed worth it as we approached the Grand Teton peak. The sun was beginning its late afternoon arc over eastern Idaho, and the rock was golden with the soft rays. The sky above us was blue, and the prospect of a successful ascent had stiffened my resolve, although I was very tired.

After nearly six hours of continuous climbing, we reached the top. The valleys and the neighboring Teton peaks were spread out before us, with the lakes sparkling beneath the Douglas firs that provide scented gateways to this mountain range. It was hard to believe we were standing on the top of a mountain that's frequently enshrouded by clouds or mist. After congratulating one another, we signed our names on the piece of paper where successful ascents are recorded.

After that, Carman was anxious to get off the mountain. He understood the rigors of scrambling down to the base camp—a trip that takes two hours under normal conditions. But today's climb down was far from normal. The hail and snowstorm had left dangerous snow and ice on the route most climbers take down the mountain.

We made our way back, sliding down a 120-foot rope and picking our way down a seemingly endless trail of boulders to the base camp.

Our guide made his way to the tent to greet his next client, the retired electrician, Harry, who had returned from St. Louis for another climb up a Teton peak.

"Sorry I'm late," Carman said, extending his hand to tomorrow's client. "Glad to see you."

Atop the Grand Teton: Wyoming's Exum School takes adventurers to lofty heights and teaches them to master mountains.

John Edward Young

GREAT BARRIER REEF

AT A DEPTH OF 75 FEET, DRIFTING BETWEEN THE SHELVES OF A CORAL canyon, life on the Great Barrier Reef begins to knock on the door of one's quiet senses.

Jacques Cousteau referred to the watery depths as "the silent world." Indeed, only the rhythmic muffled purr of bubbles flowing from our regulators interrupts the stillness.

Silent, yes, but colors and shapes unimaginable just a few short minutes ago begin to scream for attention. Fish so bizarre, in Picasso shapes and Tiffany brilliance, dart like wingless finches between branches of coral. Here on the reef, it is said, there is more life per square inch than anywhere else on earth.

Even without a single fish, the reef would lose little splendor. The soft and hard corals, made up of countless polyps, are endlessly fascinating in color, variety, shape, and size. It is these tiny, delicate animals growing from the skeletons of their ancestors that make up the reef and hold back the force of the waves.

Blizzards of silvery fish, pencil-thin, flash toward us in perfect precision, then, taking a cue from who-knows-where, change direction in a fraction of a second, catch the light, and vanish into the deep.

Drift diving with a school of yellowfin jewels.

left: *Taking a plunge into a teeming world of Picasso shapes and Tiffany colors on Australia's Great Barrier Reef.*

Great Barrier Reef off Port Douglas, Queensland, Australia.

Orange-and-white clown fish sway in a sort of seductive hula, teasing unsuspecting prey into the poisonous, soft, pink-tipped tentacles of a sea anemone. In this symbiotic relationship, the clowns have the last laugh. A mucus coating makes them immune to the anemone's deadly touch. Others are not immune.

And to think, just minutes before, the four of us were floundering about the deck in swim fins, staggering under the weight of 60-pound diving belts, struggling to keep our balance aboard the bobbing launch as assistant divemaster Terry Kennedy patiently answered our many anxious questions.

"No," he said, "you can't take any coral or anything, dead or alive, from the reef. It's a national park, remember?" And, "Yes, we will take another 45-minute dive in a different spot." And, "Yes, you have to buddy-up and stay together." And, "No, you don't *have* to wear gloves, but some of the coral is sharp and dangerous, so you better."

Then, with a nervous laugh, someone asked The Big One—"What about sharks? Any chance of seeing a shark?"

"Oh, maybe if we're lucky," Mr. Kennedy said offhandedly, without so much as looking up.

Not quite the direct, firm negative we were looking for.

Moments later we plunged into the warm waters and drifted slowly down into the azure depths.

As we made our way through a coral tunnel, Kennedy stopped to coax a six-foot moray eel from its lair with tidbits of fish. "Monty"—as Kennedy named him—was usually there, he explained. Monty would lunge out and grab a bit of fish while Kennedy tried to pet him on the head. Being in no mood to be petted that day, Monty slipped farther back to his dark lair.

Over here, Kennedy motioned, as we moved in on a lion-fish fanning its feathery orange-and-white pectoral fins. We knew enough not to get too close. Each exquisite fin houses a poisonous quill. All of us were familiar with this exotic beauty so coveted by home marine aquarists throughout the world.

Slipping deeper down to a sun-dappled coral garden, we spotted a lone three-foot giant clam lodged in the sand. A thick mantle, velvety and purple, covered its "jaws," which slowly closed as we tapped gently on one bivalve. There has never been a recorded case of anyone being caught by these "man-eaters" we were told. They simply react too slowly to threaten divers. These gentle giants live for generations, growing to over 400 pounds, and are now protected on the reef.

We hung suspended in wide-eyed amazement while a group of fish waited patiently as a thin, lithe cleaner wrasse swam in and out, from fish to fish, entering each mouth, cleaning lips, mouth, and gills, and then moving on to the next.

Even—larger fish that could eat a wrasse as an appetizer would turn and roll about with mouth open wide as the little cleaner went about its business.

The figures here are staggering: more than 1,500 identified species of fish and 350 species of coral on this 116,000-square-mile, 1,250-mile-long, 2 million-year-old reef. The Great Barrier Reef, we were told, is larger than all the man-made objects in the world put together! We swam spellbound in what amounted to little more than a drop of this underwater wilderness.

Kennedy dipped down to pick up a slippery, bulbous black sea cucumber a foot long and tossed it as we grouped together for a slow-motion game of touch football—only to be interrupted by a hawksbill turtle that came by, blinked, turned, and left looking quite bored. We dropped our slippery sea creature and gave chase.

Heron Island- 4 miles off Gladstone, Queensland, is the most southerly of the tourist resort islands. It is a true coral cay surrounded by 5 miles of reef comprising many types of coral and tropical marine life.

Five gold-and-blue angelfish drifted by as we swam between a stand of honeycomb and fan coral. One male and his four mates. If a male is lost, we learned, the dominant female quickly changes sex and takes over the harem.

Parrot fish in rainbow hues chipped away at the coral reef, spitting out tiny bits that add to the countless grains of coral sand.

Kennedy almost lost us as we followed him through a school of hundreds of midnight-blue surgeon fish, then out into a coral garden and down to a sun-dappled clearing.

Click, click, click. He tapped on his watch to attract our attention and pointed toward a large gray shadowy figure lurking ahead. A shark, as surprised as we were, if not more frightened, cut a few sweeps of its scythe-like tail and disappeared into the sea as quickly as it had appeared, leaving us with hearts throbbing in our throats.

Seconds became half an eternity.

No, the most frightening thing is not seeing a shark, I discovered. It is seeing one—and *then* not seeing it.

Kennedy's face mask hid a broad smile, but his squinty eyes, nodding head, and thumbs up signaled his delight as the four of us looked nervously about for the intruder, or worse, some of his friends. Fortunately, we saw the shark on the last minutes of our second 45-minute dive.

Up, Kennedy pointed after checking his watch, and we slowly made our ascent. "Did you see it? Did you see it? Did you see it?" we sputtered as we clamored like trained seals aboard the launch. "It must have been at least eight feet long!" "Oh, at least. Maybe 12," we argued.

"Four feet," Kennedy said coolly.

"Four feet? Come on!"

"A four-foot reef shark. Quite harmless," Kennedy said. "Water magnifies everything 25 percent."

Feeding the natives among the many varieties of soft and hard coral.

"Well I'm not telling anyone it was less than an 18-foot great white," one of the guys laughingly said as we peeled off our wet suits. Good story, we all agreed as we headed back to the catamaran.

Exhausted, excited, and relieved, we wildly embellished on how we had survived the jaws of a school of 18-foot great white sharks. Would 20 feet be overstating too much, we wondered? As for the beauty, power, and majesty of the reef, it needed no such elaboration.

Practical information

The *M.V. Quicksilver II* took us to the actual outer Great Barrier Reef. This high-speed catamaran is capable of carrying hundreds of people at a speed of 26 knots from Port Douglas to the reef, where it moors for 3 hours. The 90-minute trip out includes lectures on the reef and video and slide presentations by a marine biologist. Use of diving and snorkeling equipment is reviewed. You don't have to scuba dive. In fact, only four of the more than a hundred aboard were certified divers. To scuba dive, you must have your certified diving card with you.

Most people are content to snorkel off the side of the platform in 35-foot water. Others view the reef from the glassed-in side of a floating platform, or buzz around in the *Subsee Explorer*, a kind of submarine. You can view this watery wilderness without even getting your big toe wet. Any way you choose, the show is unforgettable, the cast is outstanding, and the set is breathtaking.

A sumptuous buffet with fresh prawns and endless salads is included in the fee, and underwater cameras are available to rent.

Contact Low Island Cruises, Port Douglas, Queensland 4871, Australia, Telephone (070) 98 5373, Telex AA48969. Port Douglas caters to divers. Qualified instructors have shops throughout the area. You can become a licensed diver in a few days.

If you want to do some homework before you go, a marine biologist on board recommended the *Reader's Digest Book of The Great Barrier Reef.*

Lodging is available and rates are moderate. I can think of no better place, however, than Silky Oaks Colonial Lodge, just 83 kilometers (50 miles) from Cairns International Airport, or 27 kilomters (half-hour drive) from Port Douglas.

Silky Oaks is a chance to see a totally different, equally fascinating side of this tropical area. Here you can live among the flora and fauna found only in this part of the world.

Moss and Theresa Hunt have cleared acres of rain forest and set up very comfortable, stilted Queensland-style cabins overlooking Mossman River Gorge. There, in the morning you can seek out a platypus searching for breakfast in a billabong, or swim among the trout while blue-crested kingfishers dive overhead. You may hand-feed bread to the wild turtles along the bank, canoe on the river, or hike through the surrounding rain forest.

right: While diving, fish will look much larger. In fact the water magnifies everything 25 percent larger.

Or just sit on your individual balcony and listen to the water and watch green birdwing and blue Ulysses butterflies flit from blossom to bud.

As Moss describes it, Silky Oaks is "living in a park—with plumbing."

One-, two-, or three-day safaris in an air-conditioned four-wheel-drive are also available. And be sure to visit the local butterfly farm. Moss will be happy take you there and be your guide along the way. He knows the names of everything that flies, crawls, or grows in the area.

Rates at Silky Oaks are moderate and include three meals a day. Both Moss and Theresa are Cordon Bleu-trained cooks, to boot.

IF YOU GO

For more details call the Australian Tourist Commission, 489 Fifth Ave. (31st floor), New York, NY 10017, (212) 687-6300 or (800) 678-8022.

93

David H. Ahl

HIKER'S PARADISE

IT WAS A CRISP, CLEAR LATE-SUMMERS DAY, THE KIND OF DAY WHEN Dad says, "Get your stuff together, we're going to the park;" the kind of day that produces five-mile traffic jams in Yosemite and Yellowstone; the kind of day that gives park rangers extra work.

As we left Wanganui early in the morning on our way to Tongariro National Park — the most visited park in New Zealand — we pondered those long traffic jams, packed trails, and strained facilities. So far we had not encountered any crowds at all — but perhaps that was because we had been caught in five days of rain on the west coast of the South Island. Now, we were on the more populous North Island, heading for Mt. Tongariro in the center — an easy half-day drive from Wellington to the south or Auckland to the north.

On the 130-kilometer (about 80-mile) drive from Wanganui to the National Park, with barely an intersection marked with a gas station and signpost, we played leapfrog with a camper, a van, and two other cars. So much for traffic jams. Another all-but-deserted 18 kilometers took us to the park headquarters — although we did have a five-minute stop to let a herd of cattle cross the road.

We learned later that New Zealand gets about 500,000 overseas visitors a year — about the same number Walt Disney World sees in one week during the

Walkers will see many sheep in New Zealand, as the 70 million sheep outnumber the people by 23 to 1.

left: Water cascades 5000 feet down Brown Falls into Milford Sound.

New Zealand and Tongariro National Park.

winter. The most popular tourist attractions, the national parks, lakes, thermal areas, and other natural wonders, get a peak of 1,000 or so visitors per day.

Total population of the country is only about 3.1 million, about the same as South Carolina, but the large land area leads to a population density of only one person per 21 acres. Moreover, better than half the population is concentrated in the three major cities — Auckland, Wellington, and Christchurch — so the countryside is sparsely populated indeed.

At the visitors center, a huge map shows a network of trails ranging in length from 3 to 50 kilometers (2 to 31 miles). The recommended time to hike the longest, the Tongariro Traverse, is four days. Huts and shelters are found about every 25 to 35 kilometers. The hut fee is NZ$7 (US$5) per night, per adult. Camping is permitted around the huts.

Prevailing moist westerly winds influence the climate of the park, which can be described as extremely variable. Frosts occur throughout the year in the higher elevations, and temperatures in the summer average 55 degrees to a maximum of 75 degrees F. No month can be described as the wettest, as most are wet.

We chose one of the shorter tramps, the Taranaki Falls Walk, about 6 kilometers long. The track starts in an area of open tussock and manuka shrub lands with patches of beech forest. Along the way, we were treated to excellent views of the symmetrical cone of Ngauruhoe Volcano, and the older, more eroded mountains of Tongariro and Pukekaikiore.

After entering the mountain beech forest, the track follows several streams. A gradual climb brought us to a broad lava flow, most of which is covered with red tussock. The far shoulder of the lava flow is at the top of a high cliff that affords a fine view of Mt. Ruapehu, Taranaki Falls (from above), and distant farmland. After a steep descent we came to the base of the falls, where the Waiere Stream spills over a 20-meter (66-foot) cliff into a pool ringed with boulders. The track then follows the stream, passing the upper and lower Cascade Falls. The forest here consists mainly of large mountain beech trees, shiny broadleaf, mountain five-finger, umbrella ferns, and small tangle coprosmas.

As the track emerges from the forest, it crosses a series of eroded gullies created by wind, rain, and frost action on the volcanic soil. Emerging from the last patch of bush, the track passes again into red tussock, leading back to Whakapapa Village and the visitors center.

It was a pleasant 2-hour tramp, more varied in terrain, perhaps, but otherwise typical of many walks that beckon hikers and naturalists throughout the country. Brochures describing area walks are available from public relations offices and motels in nearly every town in New Zealand. For example, in Greymouth, a small town on the west coast of the South Island, there are found no fewer than 12 walks, ranging from a 15-minute bush walk around Blaketown Lagoon to a half-day tramp along the Point Elizabeth Track.

The latter walk leads you through a wind-swept coastal forest, across a stretch of exposed limestone, where you can hear nothing but the pounding surf of the Tasman Sea, to a lookout at Point Elizabeth. From there you get a marvelous view of snowcapped Mt. Cook and the Southern Alps. The track then skirts the beach, follows an old mining road through the Rapahoe Scenic Reserve, and finally leads you back to the Greymouth Road.

Most of the tracks as well as the huts are maintained by the Department of Lands and Survey, or by the New Zealand Forest Service. Some towns and villages maintain local walks. We found the trails well marked and reasonably well maintained — on a par with the Appalachian Trail or Pacific Crest Trail. The flyer for each track specifies the distance, approximate walking time, and degree of difficulty.

New Zealand has no snakes or other dangerous animals, so trampers need

following pages: *Footpaths on the north side of Queenstown boast a spectacular view of Lake Wakatipu and the Remarkables Mountains.*

White water rafting on the Kawaru and Shotover rivers is challenging and exhilarating.

100

IF YOU GO

For information, contact New Zealand Tourist & Publicity, 10960 Wilshire Blvd., Suite 1530, Los Angeles, CA 90024; (213) 477-8241 or 630 Fifth Ave., Suite 530, New York, NY 10111; (212) 698-46800 or the Milford Track Office, THC Te Anau Hotel, Te Anau, New Zealand.

have no worry on that account. The country docs, however, boast a large number of unusual native trees and plants that add beauty and variety to any trek.

On the more popular tracks, the huts can be crowded at times, particularly during the December and January summer holidays. Before setting out on some of the longer tracks, you may have to register with the Forest Service. This is a safety precaution and is well advised on any track where you expect to spend more than half a day. Also, on some of the longer, more difficult tracks you may be required to travel in a group.

If you are seeking some of the finest scenery in the world, the friendliest people, and the exhilaration of the out-of-doors, head on down to New Zealand.

Practical Information

Commercially operated walking tours that provide a guide, food, and guaranteed space in the huts are available on several of the longer tracks. The most popular walk is the Milford Track. Other commercial tours on the South Island include Hollyford Valley near Milford Sound, the Routeburn Walk in Mt. Aspiring National Park, and the Abel Tasman National Park Guided Walk.

Only one guided walk is offered on the North Island, the Te Rehuwai Safari at Urewera National Park near Rotorua. Prices for these guided walks are relatively modest. For example, the Milford Track (5 days and 4 nights, the last being in a resort hotel) costs NZ$550 (US$297) and the Routeburn Walk (4 days and 3 nights) costs NZ$320 (US$175).

Some dos and don'ts in New Zealand

Do go to New Zealand as soon as possible as the US dollar is particularly strong against the New Zealand dollar.

Don't take dressy clothes. New Zealand is a casual country and you'll want comfortable clothes suitable for the out-of-doors.

Do plan to visit New Zealand for at least two weeks, preferably three or four. It's a diverse country, and it's hard to get a good feel for it in a short time.

Do try to stay several nights on a farm. You'll find it's the best way to meet the locals; moreover, you'll probably get an outstanding meal featuring local specialties.

Don't be afraid to try exotic fruits and vegetables; you'll find a taste treat in passion fruit, feijoas, kumaras, and, of course, kiwi fruit.

Do try tearooms for a light lunch. Best bets are the homemade quiches and hearty soups.

Don't tip. New Zealanders don't and they don't expect you to tip either.

Do buy what you want when you first see it. Prices don't vary much throughout New Zealand but selections do.

Do talk with New Zealanders; you'll find them remarkably well informed about world affairs and extremely friendly.

Delving into History

Exploring Dublin

'KSAN—A Remote
Indian Village Keeps Alive the
Arts of Its Ancestors

To Get Immersed in Your Vacation,
Try Diving for History

Het Loo—
"An Ugly Duckling"
Restored in the Netherlands

Winterthur

Hilary DeVries

EXPLORING DUBLIN

TO BE SURE, IT IS THE CITY'S MILLENNIUM. AS SURE, THAT IS, AS WRY, irony-attuned Dubliners can be about their home and its turbulent past—a history which actually began prior to King Mael Sechnaill II's reign, with Deyflyn, the Viking seaport on the river Liffey's south banks and goes on through centuries of enviable literary happenings and unenviable politics.

Indeed, if there is a festive mood borne on Dublin's soft summer air, it's as likely to arise from the drubbings Ireland has given England in past European Champions' Cup soccer semifinals as from any civic blarney conjured for the Irish chieftain's victory o'er the Vikings in A.D. 988.

Never mind. Any excuse for a "pairty" here will do for Dublin's 1 million own and the expected 250,000 additional visitors this year.

Manufactured or no, the Millennium has burgeoned into a year-long celebration with some 1,200 events planned (though many of them are annual occurrences anyway). This month, alone, features an international organ festival in two of Dublin's oldest churches—Christ Church Cathedral and St. Patrick's, a regatta on the Liffey, a folk music festival, and the official birthday party July 8-10, with 1,000 candles on an enormous cake in the 1,700-acre Phoenix Park.

Slow march to gentrification

Not that July holds any particular significance to the 988 victory. The month

Charming Georgian architecture in Dublin townhouses.

left: *Morning light on the Liffey.*

was chosen simply because it coincides with Dublin's yearly street fair. Such is the pleasingly ad hoc way of doing things in this Georgian city, which has weathered centuries of insurrection and is now on a slow march to gentrification.

On the skyline, construction cranes vie with cathedral spires; on the streets, horse-drawn drays and bicycles compete with Mercedeses and motorbikes. Grafton Street is now a pedestrian mall where Yankee upstarts like Ralph Lauren have opened shops alongside Dublin's ancient and honorable department stores. It's also the place where watering holes like Davey Byrne's and The Bailey, immortalized in James Joyce's *Ulysses,* are now patronized by hordes of nine-to-fivers, who crowd the sidewalks with their ties loosened and their shirt sleeves rolled, just the way the yuppie crowd on New York's South Street Seaport does.

A similar restoration is underway on Dublin Bay—the $400 million Customs House Dockside Development Project is scheduled to bring this city new hotels, offices, eateries, and plenty of Olde World charm sometime in the mid-nineties.

All this says far more about the reality of Dublin today than its Viking

Christ Church Cathedral is one of Dublin's oldest churches.

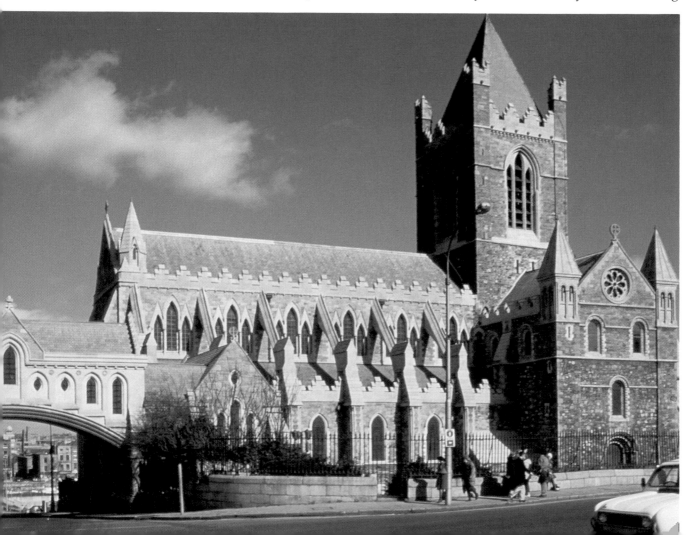

heritage, touted though it may be in the tri-color Millennium banners hung about the city. Some locals scoff at the observance, insisting that the balmy, dry summer weather and Ireland's favorable exchange rate (the dollar equivalent is $1.50 per Irish punt versus $1.80 per British pound sterling) are more conducive to a boost in tourism than the Millennium itself.

A replicated Viking village

In addition to the various events, the Millennium has inspired one important exhibit—the "Viking Experience". It's a re creation of the city's Scandinavian roots, and it's located near the original Deyflyn, in the crypts of St. Audeon's Church. The replicated Viking village there is staffed with a corps of actors performing daily tasks in the tradition of America's colonial Williamsburg: Rich in state-of-the-art verisimilitude (right down to the dubious asset of the duplicated odors of Dublin 1,000 years ago), the exhibit bears little relation to the Dublin that envelopes a visitor today.

Royal Kilmain haus.

The modern city's pleasures include the serene Georgian squares with their row upon row of picturesque doorways and cookie-cutter perfection, the smoke-filled, aged pubs, and the incessant murmur of Gaelic-cadenced conversation on every corner.

The Millennium walking tour

The most useful of the Millennium offerings? In this traveler's opinion, the thrice-daily guided tours that leave from the festival office in the Royal Hibernian Way, another luxury mall just off Grafton St. These two-hour walks acquaint the visitor with the city's high spots—Trinity College, Dublin Castle, Four Courts, St. Patrick's, the General Post Office, the site of the infamous Easter Uprisings (where you can touch the bullet holes in the walls), plus a few lesser-known treasures. Although there are also daily C.I.E. bus tours, the Millennium walk is one of the best ways to get the feel of this city, which is, one quickly discovers, an overgrown village characterized by its boisterous citizenry, very unlike its reserved neighbor, London. The Liffey, which bisects Dublin proper, is hardly Thames-sized, more like the drifting gray canals of Amsterdam.

The architecture, too, is modest. Dublin is not a city of monuments, but of doorways. The buildings are low, human-sized, and the city's dimensions barely demand a visitor's use of DART, the whisker-clean subway with its three downtown stops, or the spare taxi fleet. This is a walking city, virtually impossible to get lost in and full of interesting places to stop for local color—most notably the pubs and cafés where Dubliners congregate. Despite several new restaurants—Le Coq Hardi on Pembroke Road is most often mentioned as typical of those dishing up nouvelle Irish cuisine—most Dubliners choose to socialize and dine in the pubs and cafés. Among the best: Doheny & Nesbitt's, and any one of the Bewleys Cafés.

IF YOU GO

For more details, contact the Irish Tourist Board, 757 Third Ave., New York, NY 10017, or call (212) 418-0800.

One of the things not to miss this year (or any year) is teatime—with buttered scones and salmon sandwiches on brown bread—in the Lounge of the Shelburne Hotel, Dublin's only surviving grand hotel. The Shelburne has undergone $7 million worth of refurbishing, and the $150-a-night price seems worth it. The city's other luxury-class hotels—the Westbury and Berkeley Court—are modern buildings with different charms and amenities. Like the city itself, the 156-room Shelburne is small enough to add a wholly personal touch to its top-flight service.

Other must-sees include the *Book of Kells* in the Long Room of Trinity's Library. This illuminated calfskin manuscript—lit only by mirrors reflecting the library's natural light—is wondrous in its medieval beauty. And the looming, well-used bookcases, with their crumbling leather volumes, are evocative of the university's illustrious alumni, Yeats, Synge, Wilde, and the like.

For a touch of modern local color, catch Eamonn McThomas's weekly lectures in the lobby of the Bank of Ireland, just outside Trinity's gates. This crusty Irishman is not only the city's best-informed guide, but something of a legend and folk hero as well. His lectures, whether in the bank or on St. Stephen's Green (Wednesdays at 7 p.m. at the Grafton St. corner), are rich in history and spicy opinion. An example: "Yeats's collected poems are a beautiful 'buke' and should be kept on your bedside locker, so through the years you can reach out and read the beautiful poems."

The theater is a must see

For other linguistic pleasures, a visit to the theater is a must. It is even more accessible than London's, with only three top-flight theaters to choose from—the Gate, the Gaiety, and the Abbey. Tickets seldom exceed $15, and the annual Dublin Theatre Festival (Sept. 26-Oct. 10) will feature new productions by modern Irish playwrights Brian Friel and Frank McGuinness, along with revivals of Irish classics and new work by farther-flung companies, including the Druid and Charabanc.

Nearly every Irishman you meet—and you will have no trouble meeting a great many—will tell you a visit is incomplete without a stop in the country. DART routes to Howth and Dalkey make for easy side trips to typical Irish seaside villages. Fortunately, Wicklow Country, considered the "Garden of Ireland," is accessible via C.I.E. buses, private tour, or even taxi. Here you can visit Glendalough, or Valley of the Two Lakes, known for its exquisite natural beauty, and you can see the evocative ruins of St. Kevin's Church, an example of an early Irish barrel-vaulted church. The nearby Powerscourt House, an imposing 18th-century building on the site of the former castle of the O'Tools, offers manicured gardens with breathtaking views of Sugar Loaf Mountain.

left: *Sweethearts stroll past the General Post Office, one of Dublin's many examples of architectural variety.*

Ellen Steese

'KSAN—
A REMOTE INDIAN
VILLAGE KEEPS ALIVE
THE ARTS OF ITS
ANCESTORS

IT'S VERY IDEALISTIC—A SMALL, YET FIRST-RATE LIVING HISTORY center set miles away from anywhere. And yet it's right that it be here in Hazelton.

The 'Ksan Historic Indian Village is devoted to the culture of the Gitksan Indians of this area. It wouldn't even exist if it had not been wrenched into being by informed local people who wanted a place to display their splendid artistic heritage.

From Prince Rupert, not exactly a high-powered metropolis, you drive a good seven hours northwest—just you and the logging trucks, racing along beside the wide jade-colored Skeena River, with only mountains, mist, and trees for company. But the long drive is an appropriate introduction.

"Gitksan" means "people of the Skeena River." It was the river that made it possible for this trading people, whose main form of transportation was the canoe, to live so far inland.

'Ksan's remoteness is what makes it special. "The culture here wasn't bothered too much by white contact, so a lot of the mythology and dance remain here, while it was lost in other places," says 'Ksan Director Ron Burleigh.

The seven wooden buildings of 'Ksan are decorated with the distinctive black and red designs characteristic of west coast Indian art. They resemble the old communal houses the Gitksan Indians used to live in. Appropriately, their

A remote Indian village keeps alive the arts of its ancestors.

left: *Totem poles on the road at Kitwanga were originally carved to indicate ownership of property.*

The Gitksan Indians keep alive their splendid artistic heritage in the 'Ksan Historic Indian Village in Hazelton, British Columbia.

Intricate Chilkat blanket worn by the man on the right takes a year to weave.

backs abut the road, while the fronts look out across the Skeena at the spectacular Rocher Déboulé Mountain.

One of the first reasons for the starting of 'Ksan back in 1950 was that local people wanted a safe place—nonflammable, humidity controlled, to preserve their ancestral treasures. 'Ksan's small but up-to-the minute museum contains mostly costumes and masks—many of which are still borrowed when needed by their Indian owners for occasional ceremonies.

Today 'Ksan is much more than a museum; it's a multimedia center. Here young Indians learn to become master carvers and to perform ancient songs and dances, while older Indians give tours explaining their heritage to visitors. There's a store to market local art work, much of it of museum quality, and a small theater for performances.

Dance and song are particularly ephemeral art forms. Yet the center has managed to collect some 500 examples of these arts. To watch the 'Ksan dancers in action, you go to the Historic Village a little before 7 on a Friday night during the summer. You walk past the totem poles and cedar houses until you reach one that has a pole for a doorway. Inside there is a dimly lit stage and rows of wooden benches. During my visit they are rapidly filling up with tourists. There is a distinct and agreeable doughnut-like smell in the air of hot buckskin bread.

On one side a row of elderly Indian women is gathering. Their neat gray coiffures would be more appropriate for bridge or bingo, but they are clad in the almost military splendor of "button blankets"—navy blue wool appliquéd with red flannel and highlighted with thick rows of large pearl buttons. The Indians adapted their traditional designs to the materials that the Hudson's Bay Company (now an upmarket British Columbia department store chain calling itself "The Bay") used to sell them in exchange for furs.

A pleasant-faced young woman clasping a "speaker's pole" (which looks a bit like a miniature totem) explains that, as the audience, we represent visiting dignitaries invited to witness the induction of a new chief. "The Breath of our Grandfathers," as the show is called, is built around a ceremony as it might have appeared in 1880.

Animals are central to Indian mythology; every tribe had its own legend that connected the family's origin to an animal, after which the tribe was named. In 'Ksan, for instance, the family groups are Wolf, Raven, and Frog. So it's no surprise that many of the dances describe animals: Two beautiful, beaming little girls do a frog dance; a "mountain goat," clad from head to toe in long white fur, sways and crouches; and the most ominous was the bear, its long wooden mask gleaming menacingly in the dim light.

Most impressive of all is the dance of the running grouse. A young man in a large shawl of grouse feathers and a polished wooden helmet representing a bird, its beak pointing out over his nose, executes quick nods and swivels of the head and elbows underneath the feather cape, perfectly capturing the movements of the bird.

The English word "potlatch"—a festival with overtones of extravagance and wastefulness—isn't much liked around here. The dancers of the Performing Arts group of 'Ksan like to call their reenactment of a Gitksan get-together a "feast" or, better yet, a "celebration."

The point of the celebration is to validate hereditary rights and privileges. Potlatches, or "Yukw," as the Gitksan called them, were outlawed in 1884 in a decision that severely affected the culture of the Indians, whose myths, dance, singing, and carving were all intended to be used at these ceremonies. Over the last hundred years the Gitksan have continued to hold their feasts, quietly.

The 'Ksan dance troupe does sometimes travel. It performed at the Cultural Olympics in Montreal, for instance. And the products of `Ksan's carving school have been bought by institutions in San Francisco, Baltimore, and Kansas City, MO, and other far-flung cities as well. There are some 60 carvers in the area, and half a dozen senior carvers who give lessons.

In addition to the performances and carvings, the Gitksan women give tours, explaining displays of articles their great-great-grandparents would have used in daily life. Many of these articles are ingenious. I especially liked the boxes bent out of a single piece of wood. These, after being filled with water and hot stones from the fire, became ovens for cooking. A cedar basket looked like a rather useless object until our guide explained that the cedar expands when it is wet, closing up the holes and making the basket watertight.

About 20,000 visitors a year make their way to 'Ksan. Some of them also venture to the villages nearby—Kispiox, Kitwanga, Kitwancool—where some totems still stand in their original locations.

IF YOU GO

Hazelton can be reached by car from Prince Rupert or Prince George; the highway is excellent. Or you can take a Greyhound bus. The museum at 'Ksan Historic Indian Village is open daily in summer. The dance performance is held on Fridays during the summer months at 7:30 p.m. Tours are held from May to mid-October; admission is $4.00 (Canadian) for adults. Eating in the area is a bit of a problem. One little restaurant in Hazelton, the Mountain View, has good food. The North by Northwest Tourist Board, (P.O. Box 1030 (3840 Alfred Ave.), Smithers, B.C. V0J 2N0, Canada, (604) 785-2544), provides snappy log cabins along the highway and has maps showing where totem poles can be found.

Totem carving from huge blocks of pine.

Dely Monteser Wardle

TO GET IMMERSED IN YOUR VACATION, TRY DIVING FOR HISTORY

STAYING AT A SLEEK HIGH-RISE HOTEL, SEEING THE CAPITAL CITY from a sightseeing bus, and meeting local people only in souvenir shops isn't necessarily the most meaningful way to travel.

I've found it more fun to venture out into a country, stay for a while, and get involved. One sure way to do this is to become a volunteer on an archaeological excavation.

The greatest concentration of "digs," as they are called, is in Israel. The crescent-shaped shore along the eastern Mediterranean Sea has been inhabited for thousands of years. When you dig here, you find layer upon layer of remains from different periods, ranging from Napoleon's Egyptian campaign near the surface, down through Turkish, crusader, Islamic, Roman, Greek, Persian, Phoenician, and earlier periods—all the way back to the Stone Age.

I first worked on a dig at Tel Anafa in Galilee , up north where it isn't as hot as on southern digs in the Negev Desert. A truck took us to the site in the early morning. We dug in assigned small areas with small tools, and only down to designated levels. No random digging was allowed. If an object appeared, we called the supervisor. In the afternoons, we settled down to sort, wash, and even draw pictures of our finds.

Perhaps the most exciting finds of that dig were some pieces of an ancient

Originally an ancient Roman port, Akko is now located below sea level.

left: *Ehud Galili and part of the Mameluk treasure,the largest find of coins ever discovered on the ocean floor.*

Israel, pinpointing Caesarea.

wall covered with gold leaf. This discovery confirmed a biblical passage about "golden houses," which had not been taken literally until then.

The American-run project housed its volunteers in tiny gazebos in a park full of flowering bushes, with a little pond nearby for a swim after work. Breakfast and lunch were served from a chuck wagon. Dinner was served in the dining room of the Kibbutz Hagoshrim, on elegant Scandinavian tableware, no less.

My next dig was also in Galilee, at Akko—known to medievalists as St. Jean d'Acre during the crusades. Volunteers worked in pairs in trenches. My French companion and I had so much to talk about that the supervisor wanted to separate us, lest we neglect our work. At that time, the dig had come down to material from the Hellenistic period (Greek settlements), and I was allowed to take home some large potsherds more than 2,000 years old, which were considered surplus.

A third excursion took me into Holy Land history on an underwater sightseeing tour (with scuba-diving gear) of the sunken harbor of Caesarea, south of Akko. Here Canadian and American volunteer divers had been exploring Herod's Harbor, built in the 1st century BC, now sunken below sea level. My underwater guide on this occasion was Ehud Galili of the Center for Maritime Studies of the University of Haifa.

Galili began diving at age 11 and found artifacts underwater at 14. Later he earned degrees in geography and archaeology and made spectacular finds, such as the largest hoard of coins ever salvaged from the sea, the Mameluk treasure. Since then, Galili has become the right-hand man of Dr. Avner Raban, head of the Center for Maritime Studies, and is now running his own project, which I hope to join in early September.

In the course of a survey of the sea floor off the coast at Atlit in Galilee near Caesarea, Galili and his team discovered five submerged prehistoric villages, under mud and sand.

Last year, Galili received help from volunteer divers from the Archaeological Museum of Antibes, France, and from the Israel Underwater Society. This year he hopes to have as many volunteers as the other explorations in Galilee. Other digs there have attracted as many as 40 volunteers each, from the United States, Canada, and Europe. Professors and students have come from the University of Maryland, the University of Chicago, Texas A&M, the University of Colorado, and the University of Massachusetts, among others.

Researchers, however, have not been limited to the college crowd. Older business and professional people have come to dive and dig, some bringing along relatives.

Galili's team is very pleased with its finds from the Neolithic period (7000-4000 BC) off Atlit. Prehistoric settlements and artifacts have been found in other places, but there's much more material here. Galili has found arrowheads and axes, burned bricks, charcoal, grains and lentils, parts of a human skeleton, and bones from fish, goats, and cattle. These don't sound much like treasures. But you will understand the excitement such objects generate, once you learn what they tell us about ancient ways of life.

Before volunteers leave home, they work through a reading list provided by the Center for Maritime Studies. Before divers don a wet suit, as well as after they come out of the water, they attend archaeology sessions at the handsome University of Haifa campus about 30 miles away.

Since volunteer divers work close to shore in shallow water, don't need to swim any distance, and are constantly monitored from a raft with sophisticated equipment. They need not be experts—only certified divers with some experience.

Volunteers at Atlit are housed and fed in a nearby kibbutz. On weekends and after the session ends they can tour the country. A modest fee is charged for room and board and courses. College credit for volunteer work and study can be arranged. But not many volunteers come for credit. Most come for the joy of discovery, of helping, of really getting to know the country.

IF YOU GO

For information about the digs, write to Dr. Avner Raban/Ehud Galili at the Center for Maritime Studies, University of Haifa, Mount Carmel, Israel, 31999. El Al Israel Airlines offers a variety of special, affordable fares from the U.S.

The present day view of the fishing harbor of Akko, named after the legendary St. Jean d'Acre of the crusades.

Ellen Steese

HET LOO—
AN "UGLY
DUCKING"
RESTORED IN THE
NETHERLANDS

THE PALACE HET LOO, HOME OF THE LEGENDARY HOUSE OF ORANGE since 1688, was a tourist attraction from the start. Visitors streamed in from miles around to gaze at its fountains, its garden, its graceful exterior.

The fountains were a particular hit. Today we may take a fountain for granted, but back then, even Louis XIV of France—the king who had everything—had to make do at Versailles with jets of stagnant-smelling water pumped by horses.

At Het Loo clever engineers had a different system. The site was the lowest land in Apeldoorn, so fountains of piped-in fresh water flowed continuously down from the highlands—to the amazement of Renaissance rubberneckers.

The royal family of the Netherlands used Het Loo as a palace from the days of William III (stadtholder of the Netherlands and king of England) almost up to the time when the Dutch parliament made it a museum in 1969. From 1977 to 1984, it was closed for $81 million worth of renovations. The museum shows the relationship between the House of Orange and the history of the Netherlands, from William III to Queen Wilhelmina.

It is a grand restoration. The palace should be at the top of the Europe-bound visitor's list.

The exterior, in its brick simplicity, is very Dutch. It has been returned to its

The garden is Dutch baroque, but it will remind visitors of Versailles in its manicured formality.

left: *When restorers dug up the garden they found the original fountains underneath.*

following pages: *Detail of the graceful interior of Het Loo where the effect is splendid and spacious.*

120

Het Loo—an "ugly duckling" restored in the Netherlands.

appearance in the late 17th century, when William III came here in summer to hunt boar and to fight the French.

After Napoleon conquered Holland and installed his brother Louis at Het Loo, Louis painted the brick exterior white to make it look more French. Another story and black shutters were added later. The result had an institutional look.

Soil was thrown down to cover the fountains and parterres—areas with wonderful abstract designs in boxwood and flowers—so that a more modern garden could be planted on top.

Cultivated Renaissance people, for whom discussions of proportion were a favorite diversion, would cheer if they could see the movie today's visitors watch that explains the restoration process. In addition to footage about the history of the place, you get to see this ugly duckling turning into a swan, thanks to the army of restorers.

Het Loo leaves you exhausted, as all of the best museums do; it's an embarrassment of riches. Except for a few bare floors—where carpets weren't mentioned in the old inventories—no surface is without its tapestry or painting, silk wallpaper or plaster; no chair is without its carving, no fireplace without its assemblage of blue-and-white vases and cachepots. But the effect is splendid, not cluttered.

The sequence of rooms is a bit confusing—especially for those who have only a foggy notion of Dutch history—because the furniture styles range from late Renaissance to late Victorian. Each room is dedicated to a member of the House of Orange, and rooms are in chronological order except for the apartments of William III and his wife, Mary Stuart, which are in their original location. The English-speaking visitor should be sure to obtain a booklet in English, as the information provided in the rooms themselves is in Dutch.

The entrance is through a hall of painted gray, faux (artificial) marble.

One curator, A. M. Erkelens, points out not only that marbleizing is economical, but that "you can have all things in the manner that you want."

Be sure to pause in front of the portrait of William III, whose shrewd eyes cast a subtle sideways glance and whose face is framed by a flowing Louis XIV hairdo.

Many of the rooms feature damasks hanging loosely over bare walls. These are based on old records, according to Ms. Erkelens, who points out that "before this time they used tapestries in houses. In a way, this is a kind of damask tapestry."

Early inventories helped curators to discover the original colors in each room. To ascertain the quality—which is exquisite—they received permission from Queen Elizabeth II to study the damask at Great Britain's Hampton Court Palace. The room of William III has a brilliant orange tapestry, in honor of Orange, the original family principality in the south of France; the royal blue of the bed hangings represents the color of the House of Nassau, a family possession in Germany.

The public rooms are spacious, the private rooms smaller. Queen Mary Stuart's snuggery is no larger than a good-sized closet, but it has a charming fireplace bearing her collection of blue-and-white porcelain.

According to E. Elzenga, another curator, the restoration process at Het Loo was full of surprises. One was the discovery that the boards of the original trompe l'oeil ceilings had simply been turned over and painted on the other side, leaving the design intact. "We could have reconstructed the whole house with the original paint, but we still didn't have the furniture," Mr. Elzenga explains. The French Army took everything away in 1795, "so this restoration is a combination of reconstruction and making compromises."

Another surprise for restorers was to find that when they dug up the garden, the original fountains were still underneath. The garden is Dutch baroque, but it will remind visitors a lot of Versailles in its neatness, its pointed fir trees, its statues and colonnades, and in the elaborate whirling designs in boxwood, a sort of botanical marquetry.

Many of the statues are copies of those at Versailles. A notable difference, however, is that the parterres in the gardens are square, rather than elongated, which gives the garden an intimate feeling of enclosure, as opposed to the French preference for long vistas.

All of the present plantings would have been here at the end of the 17th century. Walter Harris, physician in the English court of King William III, wrote a book in which he gave a plant-by-plant description of the garden. He listed, among "flowers which successfully blow according to the seasons of the year:" ranunculus, tulips, hyacinths, anemone, narcissus, summer poppies, gillyflowers, lark-heels, sunflower, Indian cresses, stock-rose, and marigolds.

The statue of Venus in the center of the garden was a tribute to Mary Stuart, says Elzenga, while the fountains symbolized the power of the king.

IF YOU GO

Apeldoorn is about 50 miles east of Amsterdam and can be reached by train or car. Driving in Holland is easy, the roads excellent and well marked. There are two exhibitions in the wings of the palace. One features heraldry and related objects. The other features paintings, prints, and documents. Both are open afternoons. The orientation movie is available in English on request, and tours are given in English as well as Dutch. There are also occasional concerts. For travel details to Holland contact The Netherlands National Tourist Office, 355 Lexington Ave., New York, NY 10017, or call (212) 370-7360.

Rear view of palace: even Louis XIV didn't have a fresh–water fountain like this.

John Edward Young

WINTERTHUR

WITH ITS LUSH ENGLISH GARDEN SURROUNDING A PSEUDO-FRENCH chateau capped by a Spanish tile roof, Henry Francis du Pont's 980-acre "country farm," Winterthur, seems an unlikely home for the foremost collection of American furniture and decorative arts anywhere.

But the nearly 200 furnished rooms in this huge stuccoed estate sweep across two centuries of home furnishings—from about 1640 to 1840, a period of outstanding American craftsmanship and creativity. Everything from the clean, ascetic style of the Shakers to the warm, sumptuous Queen Anne period is represented.

To previous generations of the family, Winterthur (whose Swiss-German name is pronounced Winter-tour) was simply a comfortable house in the country. But du Pont's impeccable taste, considerable curiosity, and meticulous attention to detail have made Winterthur *the* American historic home of taste and style.

Long before Americans were encouraged to "look for the Union label," Henry Francis du Pont (1880-1969) was gathering those things exclusively "made in America." The exceptions—Oriental rugs, brasses, porcelain, some silver, and chandeliers—were the appointments traditionally imported or simply not yet available in the New World.

left: *Many years of planning to place the furniture, rugs, pictures, mirrors, and small objects have created the harmony seen in the Chinese parlor.*

124

The Winterthur estate lies nestled in the northern part of Delaware within an easy distance from Pennsylvania, New Jersey, and Maryland.

As a youngster, du Pont spent an idyllic childhood romping through the vast acres of Winterthur, collecting birds' eggs and nests, as well as various mineral specimens, and developing the family's deep passion for gardening.

After marrying and living away for a time, he and his wife, Ruth, and two daughters returned here after du Pont inherited the "farm." Though as a young man he loved the virgin forests and carefully planned gardens that surround the Great House, he didn't share the family's taste in furniture. He "heartily disliked" the dark Empire-style veneered mahogany he grew up with.

Later he declared, "I decided we would not have a piece of it." Instead, he searched beyond the walls of Winterthur for fine period pieces.

Unlike many of his wealthy contemporaries, he had little interest in sports, and chose instead to devote much time to collecting furniture and art. Rather than spend hours on the family tennis courts trying to improve his serve, he traveled to the great homes, gardens, and museums of Europe, refining his eye and broadening his tastes.

As the collection expanded, the space on the estate that once had been devoted to recreation fell to du Pont's consuming interest. The billiard and ping pong rooms, bowling alley, and squash and badminton courts soon housed New York Chippendale chairs, Pennsylvania German cabinets, and the expertly crafted works by Duncan Phyfe, John Townsend, and John Goddard.

Crediting himself with what a noted museum curator referred to as "being born with a 'seeing eye' fit…to pick and choose," du Pont noted rather immodestly, "…it is fortunate that I seem to notice everything that is attractive and beautiful." Winterthur stands today as evidence.

Inside the house, hand-carved eagles soon replaced the moth-eaten stuffed birds of his childhood. Robins' nests gave way to nests of Chinese export bowls, and du Pont's love of minerals expanded to a collection of marble fireplaces.

Although du Pont had his own aesthetic leanings, he became increasingly concerned with regional and historical accuracy and more selective in his acquisitions, as well as with whom he discussed them.

As the hobby grew, so too did Winterthur. A huge wing, added in the late 1920s, tripled the size of the already enormous home. Soon friends, relatives, and strangers began contributing their treasured heirlooms. One ecstatic donor went so far as to suggest that giving an object to Winterthur "was like having it go to Heaven."

Regardless of what was offered, du Pont carefully decided what pieces to accept, and which brass candle snuffer would rest on which William and Mary table.

A wide-eyed reporter once asked him who his agent was. "You're looking at him," answered du Pont.

In the evolution from home to museum, two pieces of American furniture are considered pivotal to du Pont's collection. One rather modest example —a plain walnut chest from Pennsylvania, inlaid with the date 1737—is said to be the first piece he actually bought.

The other piece caught his fancy early on. During a trip to New England, he became "fascinated by the colors of a pine dresser filled with pink Staffordshire plates." This cupboard, in the home of Mrs. J. Watson Webb of Shelburne, Vt., along with its pink plates, was not to be his until years later after Mrs. Webb's death. Fortunately, patience was one of du Pont's virtues. These two pieces are now among the items on view.

And du Pont didn't just gather furniture and push it against any available wall at random. Whole rooms of handpainted wall coverings, carved wooden paneling and moldings, floors, even plaster ceilings—from places ranging from early New England homes to Georgia plantations—were carefully removed and reconstructed here to give a sympathetic look to objects within a room. "Sometimes you have to buy the whole house to get what you want," du Pont once ranted.

Settings of Chinese export porcelain are elegantly placed on dining tables as if ready for use, or perched in lofty open cabinets. Some pieces are exquisitely decorated with flowers and bucolic scenes; others are amusingly mismarked. One set of export dinnerware shows the American founding fathers with distinctly Oriental features. Another, emblazoned with the American eagle, was supposed to display the motto "e pluribus unum". It came back, "e rlupib umum."

Nothing, though, was quite as embarrassing as the set a British family ordered with their family motto, "Think and Thank;" we may be amused, but certainly they were not, when it came from China marked "Stink and Stank."

For all the staggering number of formal parlors, dining and bed rooms, sitting rooms and kitchens, Winterthur is quite easy to absorb. Most rooms are relatively small and cheerfully bright. All are inviting. This is partly due to the way rooms and appointments are presented. You're not likely to suffer from "museum syndrome," as nothing is viewed "under glass." Each room opens like a three-dimensional, Technicolor, stereoscopic picture of the past. There's a feeling, as you enter a room, that family and guests of the period have heard your footsteps and quietly adjourned to the next room.

This is no mere coincidence. Each room was put together, with du Pont's keen interest, in a harmonious flow. His close attention to detail is evident. When he decided where something should go, the spot was marked with a tack, and the piece stayed there. His terms were explicit: "It has taken many years of careful planning to place the furniture, rugs, pictures, mirrors, and all small objects in

126

exactly the places they are now.... I wish them to remain precisely as I have placed them, and on no condition do I want the arrangement to be changed by even an inch."

Thirty rooms here are now "frozen" to du Pont's expressed wishes.

Yet, each perfectly appointed room embraces you as you enter. No one piece of furniture, no matter how monumental in size, needlessly attracts or dominates. Every object fits like the piece of a puzzle in one large historical panorama, leaving the impression that, although nothing stands out, a gaping hole would be left if any one thing were removed. Here again is du Pont's attention to detail. He explained, "It's one of my first principles that if you go into a room...and right away see something, then you must realize that it shouldn't be in the room."

du Pont was particular, too, about the way Winterthur was presented to visitors. He could strike more than a little fear in a guide by slipping in with a tour unannounced. He admonished guides not to "talk too much, except in reply to questions that may be asked." He preferred that there be no set talks about any one room.

Today a visitor shouldn't come here thinking to escape a sense of national pride. Every piece of Americana—from the large spreading wooden eagle in the conservatory with its outstretched wings spanning 15 feet, to the small, delicately inlaid ones topping the legs of a Federal dining table, and the gleaming silver Paul Revere tankards, or the Copley paintings, and the heroic etchings of Washington, Franklin, and Jefferson—all convey a sense of patriotism that leaves few persons unmoved.

The complete balance of all the decorative arts complement each other in this formal dining room.

Memorable Voyages

Transcanal Cruise

Voyage Up the Volga

Good-bye "Real World,"
Hello Mayreau

Sailing the Greek Isles—
Where Myths Become Reality

Steaming Up the
Norwegian Coast:
Breathtaking Vistas,
Native Charm

Sonia W. Thomas

TRANSCANAL CRUISE

A CRUISE THROUGH THE PANAMA CANAL ATTRACTS A VARIETY OF passengers.

Steve Skovran from Warren, Ohio, is here for his second time. "I came through the first time in early 1946 as a Navy crewman aboard the destroyer *U.S.S. Woodworth*. World War II was just over, and we were taking the ship back to the East Coast to be mothballed," he says.

This time Skovran brought his wife, Helen, to show her the workings of the canal from the deck of the *Pacific Princess.*

Other veterans who went through the canal in WWII are back with their families. The rest of us have signed on to take a look at one of the major engineering feats of all time—or simply to soak up the sun and relax in the luxury of the ship seen on TV's "Love Boat" series.

Transiting the canal

On transit day, everyone is up at dawn for the nine-hour-plus trip from the Pacific to the Caribbean. A pilot arrives in his droning boat to help the captain guide our ship through the canal. From that time until our transit is completed 50 miles later, there's much to see.

The *Pacific Princess* is navigating the transcanal route between Acapulco, Mexico, and San Juan, Puerto Rico. The cruise takes 10 nights going east and 11

Traffic in the two narrow lanes of the locks is one-way—west to east in the morning and east to west in the afternoon.

left: The Pacific Princess *makes the canal transit in nine hours.*

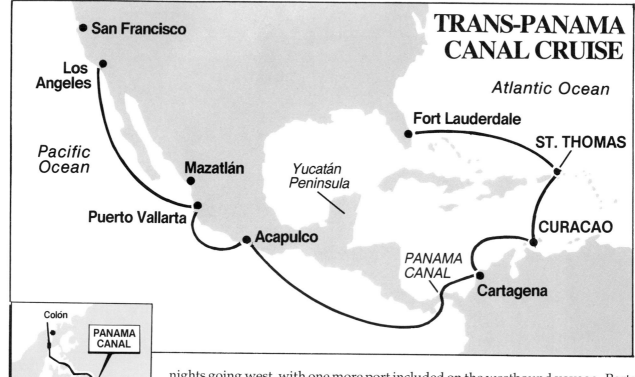

TRANS-PANAMA CANAL CRUISE

Atlantic Ocean

Pacific Ocean

San Francisco

Los Angeles

Mazatlán

Puerto Vallarta

Acapulco

Yucatán Peninsula

Fort Lauderdale

ST. THOMAS

CURACAO

PANAMA CANAL

Cartagena

Colón

PANAMA CANAL

Lake Gatun

Route of cruise from Acapulco through the Panama Canal to San Juan.

nights going west, with one more port included on the westbound voyage. Ports on the way are Acapulco, Mexico, Cartagena, Colombia; and the Caribbean islands of Aruba, Martinique, St. Thomas, and Puerto Rico. Passengers don't go ashore in Panama but see Panama City in the distance from the canal.

The story of the canal's construction is compelling, and a preview slide show acquaints passengers with the details.

As early as 1534, Charles I of Spain had ordered a survey for a proposed sea route through the Isthmus of Panama. Yet it wasn't for three more centuries (1880) that France began work on a canal. Twenty years later, the French gave up, because the problems of financing the venture and dealing with the diseases that troubled the workers seemed overwhelming.

Then, in 1903, the United States and Panama signed a treaty, and the U.S. started planning how to accomplish the project. A year later the U.S. purchased the rights and properties from the French Canal Company and started work. Ten years and $387 million later, the canal was opened for ship traffic.

Three major problems were overcome: sanitation, engineering, and organization. The first obstacles undertaken were to clean up the area and control the mosquitoes and related diseases. Once that was done, the engineering problems could be dealt with. These included digging through the high land of Central America's continental divide, fashioning the largest earth dam built to that time, and designing and constructing the largest locks and gates ever made.

President Theodore Roosevelt said it could only have been done through "American ingenuity." Three men are credited with spearheading the task: engineer John F. Stevens and two administrators, Col. George W. Goethals and Col. William C. Gorgas, who took the lead in solving the health problems.

The French engineers had conceived of a sea-level canal and failed; the U.S. engineers saw the necessity for raising ships above sea level, via a series of locks. As a result, ships transiting the canal are raised 85 feet to pass through a lake, and then they are lowered again to sea level.

The man-made portion of the canal consists of channels at each ocean end, three sets of locks, and the 23-mile-long Gatun Lake in the middle, formed by a dam on the Chagres River. The water in the locks is gravity-fed, with no mechanical pumps. So the pressure of the lake water is essential to the operation. From the ship you can watch the water lowering in one lock as it rises in the other at the rapid rate of 39 inches a minute.

Pacific Princess *in the port of* St. Thomas

During the transit, a guide on board explains the details over a loudspeaker to passengers who have gathered on the deck to watch. Most of us are there, elbowing our way to the rail in order to snap photos, only to find later that a lot of heads and arms show up in them.

For safety reasons traffic in the two narrow parallel lanes of the locks is one-way—west to east in the morning and east to west in the afternoon.

The *Pacific Princess* is paired up with a large grain carrier, the *Sunny Glorious*, and it's fascinating to watch the two ships inch forward as water moves from one lock to the other to float us through.

Canal traffic is heavy, and ships must reserve their time slots in advance. Passenger ships, which have priority, pay one of the largest fees. According to the guide, "The tariff for the *Pacific Princess* is about $40,000. The highest fee paid is by the *Queen Elizabeth II*—at $89,154.62; the lowest was by author/adventurer Richard Halliburton, who paid 36 cents to swim through the canal in 1928."

One is struck by the vulnerability of this vital, narrow shipping passage, which saves ships so much time and money. Also, with the seeming importance of the U.S. support system and presence along the route, especially when one considers that the canal reverts to Panamanian sovereignty in the year 2000.

Tankers, container ships, and auto carriers lie at anchor in the Pacific, Caribbean, and Gatun Lake, waiting their turn to go through. At wide places in the lake and in the canal between the locks we pass ships going the opposite way, which will wait their turn at the locks beyond. Surprisingly, we pass small sailboats being shepherded through in "pods" of five or more at a time.

By the end of the day, passengers are ready for a rest. It's a lot of hard work to keep up with what's going on at both bow and stern—with locks opening in front and closing behind—not to mention watching the sturdy locomotives that pull the ships through the locks. Then there's the toll of a day in the tropical heat and humidity.

Inside the *Pacific Princess*

That's when you enjoy going inside the air-conditioned ship to find something cool to drink. On the *Pacific Princess*, that's easy. There are at least six lounges on several decks where you can get cool drinks at almost any time of day. And there are two pools on deck, which offer snack service throughout the day.

"The Love Boat" lives up to its screen image in almost every way. Except, come to think of it, I haven't seen any budding romances on board, nor any celebrities on this Easter Week cruise, though we do have three clergymen on board to conduct religious services.

Yet the familiar settings are here: the sun deck with its pool and mermaid statue, the tasteful decor, and the familiar circular staircase where passengers pose for photos to take to the friends back home. Our captain, Michael Bradford, is every bit as gracious as TV captain Merrill Stubing (played by Gavin MacLeod). And Cruise Director Jim Everett and his staff are as friendly as any seen on screen.

In fact, cordiality is the keynote of the *Pacific Princess* cruise experience. Everything possible is done to make us feel, in Captain Bradford's words, like "one of the family."

The *Pacific Princess* and her sister ships are part of the P&O Lines (Peninsular and Oriental Steam Navigation Company), which is celebrating its 150th anniversary this year.

According to Deputy Captain David Brown, "Like a lot of other lines, the P&O, famed for the long voyages that carried British passengers to India and the Orient beginning in 1837, nearly went under in the late sixties. That's when air travel creamed passengers off the long-distance routes.

"Short ocean cruises had been introduced by some ships to fill the gap between the seasons," Captain Brown continues. "Suddenly, the passenger lines realized that, to stay in business, they would have to operate differently. So the shorter cruise was tried all year long. It not only succeeded, but gave birth to an industry which is growing fast today."

Cuisine on the *Princess*

The *Pacific Princess* offers passengers three enormous meals a day. The cuisine is intercontinental, with an Italian flair. The menu varies each day with a different theme for dinner: British, Italian, French, and American, with a lights-out finale parade of waiters carrying flaming Baked Alaska. All meals are served with a flourish by the well-trained, mostly Italian staff. And, if three square meals aren't too much for one day, you can take tea and sweets at 4 p.m. or go to the snack buffet at 11:30 p.m.

Activities on board

Entertainment is, of course, an important feature on any cruise ship. But it's especially so on the eastbound transcanal cruise, where the ship is under way three days with no ports of call between Acapulco and the canal.

Activities are planned throughout the day for anyone who chooses to get involved. They include dance, exercise, and crafts classes, bingo both morning and afternoon, and a casino open afternoons and evenings. On each cruise there's an instructor who teaches bridge to beginners and helps more advanced players improve their game.

Lectures and slide shows include talks on ports to be visited, details about the ship, a cooking lesson and tour of the galley, and a fashion show. Current movies are shown several times a day. Then, you can find shuffleboard and skeet shooting on a rear deck. Joggers and walkers can exercise on the top sun deck, where 18 times around equals one mile.

Live shows are presented before and after the late sitting in the dining room.

If you want to just relax, there's plenty of deck space and time for reading, cooling off in one of the pools, or napping in the sun or shade.

Dress on board is casual during the day, with shorts, slacks, and sports attire acceptable anywhere. On some evenings casual dress is also encouraged. There are three formal nights, however, when guests can break out their long dresses and dinner jackets, though shorter-length dresses, and suits or sports jackets and ties, are equally acceptable.

IF YOU GO

For more information about schedules and cost for the Pacific Princess Lines ships contact your travel agent.

Captain, crew, and passengers watch as lock fills with water at the rate of 39" per minute.

Phyllis Krasilovsky

VOYAGE UP
THE VOLGA

A VOLGA RIVER CRUISE OFFERS A MOST LUXURIOUS AND UNHURRIED opportunity to get acquainted with the Soviet Union, past and present.

The river is a ribbon that acts as the cultural, as well as physical, boundary between Europe and Asia. The Russian revolutionary tradition was born along its shores along with Lenin, whose birthplace, Ulyanovsk, is beside the river. His statues and billboard-sized portraits dwarf the central squares of every town and city we encountered.

Like the Chinese, the Russians make sure tourists see as much as possible. Typical bus tours for Volga cruise-boat passengers include visits to youth camps, circuses, hospitals, day-care centers, museums, and monuments—especially monuments. Commemorative markers tend to dominate the country's parks and highways.

Shifting scenes of the Volga

The Volga itself has a singular beauty, yet an enormous variety of scenery. Unlike the Mississippi, the Nile, the Rhine, or the Amazon, it rarely narrows, except for access to 13 locks and the place where it diverges from the Don into a narrow canal. Most traffic on the river consists of hydrofoils, boats hauling logs, and freighters marked with the ubiquitous red hammer and sickle.

In some stretches, the Volga is so wide that its vague, distant shores appear

The Alexander Pushkin *cruising the Volga, offers spacious decks for sunbathing travelers.*

left: *The locks can be quite elegant with walls bordered by gilded Parisian-like streetlamps.*

136

as mirages over large, silver expanses of water. Fishermen and swimmers use its sloping concrete embankments for their pleasures. In some places, craggy yellow cliffs, similar to those along the Yugoslav coast, mark its edges.

But sometimes one sees verdant hills, birch forests, and small Doctor Zhivago-like villages, with their clusters of colored "gingerbread" houses. Farmhouses and barns of unpainted, weather-washed gray wood make one think of the sets for *Fiddler on the Roof.*

In contrast, ornate two- and three-stored Victorian boathouses of mint green, electric blue, and garish pink with white gingerbread-trimmed windows resemble frosted cakes.

Most of the locks are very elegant, with walls bordered by gilded Parisian-like streetlamps. The approach at twilight can be a memorable experience. After the boat arrives between towering walls in the lock, the water slowly rises. Then—as if they were scrolling downward on a television screen—flowers, trees, and houses suddenly appear, with rooftops last. When the lock opens, the boat sails out into the widened river, whose shores are lit with twinkling lights, and sudden cool breezes fill the decks.

Ten days on the *S.S. Alexander Pushkin* is considered the highlight of the International Cruise Company's three-week "Lands of the Golden Horde" tour of Russia. And this traveler would agree that the charms of the floating hotel win out over the exotic attractions of Leningrad, Moscow, Armenia, and Georgia.

The 1,100-mile Volga cruise is not a typical fun-and-sun voyage, of course. Activities are controlled by Intourist, the national tourist agency, with set hours for relaxing, swimming, and entertainment.

Our group was enchanted from the start. That was when Clavdia, the diminutive entertainment director for our cruise, clad in a folk costume, welcomed everyone aboard with the traditional cakelike bread and salt. Spirited music by a three-piece combo accompanied passengers up the gangplank of the white, Austrian-built vessel.

Once on board, we discovered identical picture-windowed staterooms, decorated in cheerful prismatic colors. There was ample room for storage, plus showers and makeup tables. A complete inspection of the ship revealed that all public rooms were equally spotless and attractive.

Service in the dining room was good, but passengers sometimes had to cling to dishes to prevent an over-zealous waitress from whisking them away. The fish, salad, and soup courses, as well as cakes intended for dessert were frequently put upon the table all at one time.

The food was delicate and fresh, featuring such Russian specialties as stuffed cabbage, borsch, blinis, stroganoff, and Siberian stew, as well as vegetarian dishes. Caviar appeared several times, in mounds of red, black, and gray.

Promptly at 7 a.m., a broadcast through cabin loudspeakers opened with recorded sea gulls and folk music, then the tour program for the day, selected news, and an invitation to exercise on the sun deck.

Breakfast, where the starched linen napkins stood at attention, was served promptly at 8.

The pleasures of strolling along the shore, whether through a birch wood or a busy terminal dock, awaited early risers. In Rostov-on-Don, we found people on the quay to be friendly and smiling and not averse to posing for pictures.

Russia's Young Pioneers youth group are getting a special view of history.

138

Perhaps because it was the holiday season, many of them were indulging in ice cream before 9 a.m.!

As a large pleasure boat docked, a troupe of young ballerinas dressed in tutus performed a welcoming dance for us to an accordionist's music. It was an idyllic scene that diminished the specter of arms races and nuclear tests.

On-board activities included a Russian tea party, where costumed waitresses served the tea from an impressive samovar and passed around chocolate bears and cookies.

Also features were a blini-tasting party, a passengers' amateur night of entertainment, daily Russian-language lessons, Intourist movies on art and travel in the USSR, and three lectures by Prof. Jonathan Sanders of the Russian Institute of Columbia University.

Sanders's topics included "Cossacks and Cowboys" and "NATO and Plato," and he was always available to answer questions on any facet of Soviet life.

Islands, memorials along the way

The day spent at Don Cossack Island turned out to be a distinctly Russian swimming experience and an opportunity to watch citizens at play. Half-hour troika rides operated by thatch-haired costumed boys provided a bit of Chekohovian atmosphere.

Variety and contrasts abound on the 1,100 mile trip on the Volga River. Tbilisi, Russia's answer to New Orleans, offers donkey rides through its beautiful park.

139

A distinctive Russian bouillabaisse was served, and everyone got to keep their wooden spoons, painted with folklore figures.

Another island day, this one set aside for relaxation, included a shish kebab picnic as well as swimming. But the highlight was a hilarious King Neptune musical, presented by several of the passengers, under Clavdia's direction. Clavdia didn't speak a word of English, except for the command "Applowse!"—to which everyone responded with vigor. Otherwise, she managed to communicate with place cards and her expressive eyes.

Of all the excursions that focused on war memorials and Lenin monuments, the most impressive was Mamayev Hill in Volgograd, the scene of fierce fighting in World War II. Today the hillside is covered with awesome statues, particularly *Victory*, a torch-bearing woman who seems to dwarf New York's Statue of Liberty.

Lenin's house in Ulyanovsk contains intriguing artifacts, such as an oil lamp attached to two globes. When lit, the lamp shows the rotation of the moon around the earth. Ulyanovsk is a highlight for the aesthete because of the charming gingerbread houses on the surrounding streets.

The kremlin (walled city) in Kazan, the 700-year-old capital of the Tatar Soviet Socialist Republic, is also filled with architecturally striking buildings, though some might think its star-filled blue onion domes are straight out of Disneyland.

Personal visits, unhurried pace

In addition to sightseeing, there were people-to-people encounters like the Friendship Society party we attended in Togliatti, the visit we made to a youth camp in the birch-forested outskirts of Kazan, and our trip to a day-care center in Ulyanovsk.

These offered enjoyable and valuable opportunities for firsthand knowledge and understanding.

The frequent tours from the ship seemed tranquil in comparison to the pace of sightseeing elsewhere in the world. No one can complain about missing any highlights in the cities we visited, except for the houses of worship.

Among the other sights were Leningrad's Hermitage Museum and Peterhof Palace; Moscow's Red Square, Kremlin, and Novo-Devichly Convent; stupendous views of Mt. Ararat; the superb monastery at Garni outside of Yerevan; and the city of Tbilisi, Russia's answer to New Orleans, with its balconied houses interspersed with magnificent baroque palaces, art galleries, and an opera house.

The overwhelming encounters with people and their customs and culture make this a particularly worthy trip. Its chief side benefits were the fostering of a better understanding and a heightened personal awareness of the visitors' more privileged lives at home.

Marilynne Rudick

GOOD-BYE "REAL WORLD," HELLO MAYREAU

THERE ARE THREE WAYS TO GET TO CANOUAN, THE GLIMMERING gold and green gem of the Grenadines. One way is to hitch a ride on the twice weekly inter-island mailboat. The second is to scare up a small plane. The third, and certainly the most pleasant, is by private yacht. We chose the third—a comfortably outfitted 43-foot, sloop-rigged Beneteau. In our case, the yacht was merely ours for a 10-day charter, long enough to sail to Canouan and the other islands, between St. Vincent and Grenada, that make up the Grenadines (geographically a part of the Windward Islands). Aboard our boat, the *Zachari*, we leapfrogged from island to island.

And while the three-dozen islands are clustered together in a 50-mile string, they often seem worlds apart. There's Mustique, peopled by the jet set; Mayreau, undiscovered and native; and the Tobago Cays—inhabited only by brilliantly colored fish.

We chartered our boat from the Moorings, one of half a dozen charter boat companies in the Windwards. We opted for a bare boat, which meant that the six of us—three couples—captained and crewed the vessel ourselves. But for those who don't know port from starboard, the charter companies will provide a captain and crew.

Sailing in the Grenadines is not for everyone. If you embrace the Holiday

left: *On board in the Grenadines: dinner flambé.*

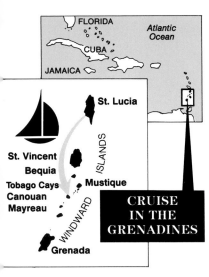

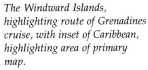

The Windward Islands, highlighting route of Grenadines cruise, with inset of Caribbean, highlighting area of primary map.

Inn's concept of "no surprises," or seek glitter and gourmet restaurants, go elsewhere. But if you've lamented that you got to Hawaii after James Michener, try the Grenadines.

We had our share of surprises. The Moorings boasts of weather that's 80 degrees and sunny. But we left on our first sail from St. Lucia's Marigot Bay in the rain. Trapped by the tall volcanic mountains, the Pitons, rain dogged us for much of "the long passage"—55 miles down the coast of St. Lucia, past St. Vincent to Bequia. But when we'd navigated it successfully, we congratulated ourselves on having accomplished the sailing equivalent of a triathlon.

We dried out in Bequia, an island with a long tradition of fishing and whaling. We browsed in boutiques and uncovered Bequia's cottage industry. Local craftsmen, with the most rudimentary of hand tools, turn out meticulously carved and intricately decorated models of boats. In the afternoon, we collapsed on Princess Margaret's beach to enjoy our first sunshine. At night we took our dinghy into town to visit a "jump-up"—an island equivalent of a disco—albeit with a steel band.

When we left Bequia the next day, we left civilization. St. Lucia and Bequia are large islands with the accompanying "urban" hassles of crowded harbors. From Bequia, we sailed backward in time. As we pointed our boat and headed for places we'd never received postcards from, the pace slowed.

Canouan, with hills the color of Van Gogh's palette, was as much a getaway place as you're likely to find. Two small hotels accommodate tourists. We walked to "town"—a tiny post office and cinder-block sometime movie theater. A women-only road crew was fixing the main road for traffic that consisted of bikes, donkeys, and an occasional motorcycle.

At Tobago Cays, we enjoyed some of the Caribbean's best snorkeling. The huge, shallow reefs of fantail and brain coral—just off the three Cays—are perhaps the best place for a beginning snorkeler. Not only are the fish abundant and diverse, but the often waist-deep reef makes it easy to stand up and reconnoiter.

My two favorite islands were probably Mayreau and Petit St. Vincent—opposite worlds. Mayreau won my vote for charm and isolation. The island is a canvas of tropical colors and images—lime green and hot pink houses—and gardens with vegetables and pink and red flowers. At the very top of the island, there's a small stone church, with goats grazing in the churchyard.

Petit St. Vincent, an island resort, lies at the other end of the pampering spectrum. This 100-acre resort island caters to just 44 guests—housed in 22 cottages scattered amid the island's palms and sea grapes and attended to by a staff of 70. Rope hammocks, protected from the sun by thatched roof huts, are scattered about the powder sand beach that rims the island.

One of the pleasures of a cruising vacation is its simplicity. The boat is both your transportation and hotel. There is no concern with what to wear. Bathing suits, shorts, and T-shirts suffice, with only one slightly dressy outfit for the fanciest restaurants. We had arranged for the Moorings to "split provision" our boat. They provided amply for all our breakfasts, lunches, and snacks, and six of our ten dinners. For our onboard meals, we relied heavily on the charcoal grill, hung off the stern. We left St. Lucia with a large stalk of bananas— the island's chief crop— and cooked up endless variations: Our dwindling stalk became our calendar, measuring the days left until our return to the "real world." On our nights out, we splurged at Petit St. Vincent and the Cotton House on Mustique, an elegantly restored 18th-century plantation, and had a more native meal at Captain Hook's at Soufrière Bay in St. Lucia.

Often what is most memorable about sailing in the Grenadines are the times you did nothing or close to nothing. Such times were spent sipping a cold drink on deck while watching the long afternoon fade into dusk, then the gaudy sunset show followed by the dizzying spectacle of the Milky Way. There was the nightly search for the green flash—a streak of green light on the horizon that's said to follow the Caribbean sunset. Few pleasures equal snorkeling very slowly through clear turquoise water amid a million tiny silvery fish, sailing alongside a school of playful dolphins, or watching the rain give way to a vibrant rainbow.

Our final destination was St. Lucia's Soufrière Bay. Once our boat was safely tied to a palm tree, we took a side trip by cab to Soufrière Volcano. The bubbling pools of lava, the hazy yellow clouds of sulfurous steam, the accompanying rotten-egg smell, and the stained green and yellow "moonscape" seemed to provide a fitting, if somewhat ironic, finale to our trip. The now dormant volcano was a vivid reminder of the violent origins of these islands that had provided us with such peace and serenity.

Figuring costs: Renting our 43-foot Beneteau, one of the smaller, less expensive boats offered by the Moorings, costs $442 a day in the high winter season, $186 off season. Split provisioning (that means breakfasts, lunches, and four out of seven dinners) costs $18 per person per day.

Planning your cruise: The following guides are helpful: Chris Doyle's *Sailor's Guide to the Windward Islands* (Cruising Guide Publications, Box 13131, Station 9, Clearwater, FL 33519 (813) 797-9576). Jill Bobrow and Dana Jinkins's *St. Vincent and the Grenadines: A Plural Country* (Norton).

IF YOU GO

Chartering a yacht: These companies arrange both bare boat and crewed charters and assist with travel arrangements; departures are generally from St. Lucia or St. Vincent: The Moorings USA, Suite 402, 1305 US 19 South, Clearwater, FL 34624, (800) 535-7289). Stevens Yachts, 50 Water St., South Norwalk, CT 06854, (800) 638-7044). Caribbean Sailing Yachts Ltd., Box 491, Tenafly, NJ 07670, (800) 631-1593). Ann-Wallis White, 326 First St., Annapolis, MD 21403, (301) 263-6366.

Sonia W. Thomas

SAILING THE GREEK ISLES— WHERE MYTHS BECOME REALITY

THE MERE MENTION OF THE GREEK ISLANDS CONJURES UP A PICTURE of sun-splashed land jutting abruptly out of lapis-blue water. This image makes you want to drop everything and go—to see for yourself.

If you do plan a Greek islands trip, you may find yourself on one of several Greek-owned Epirotiki ships, a line that began back in 1954. "That was the year that Epirotiki teamed up with the new National Tourist Organization to convert a small liner, the *M.V. Semiramis*, into a cruise ship," said Andreas Paliuras, purser of the *M.T.S. Oceanos*. He added, "Its first cruise carried 150 passengers, including several journalists, who loved it and went home to write about it." The experiment proved to be most successful.

Now, of the nearly 30 cruise ships sailing in the Aegean and Mediterranean waters, 11 are owned by Epirotiki.

My husband and I sailed from Piraeus, the port of Athens. On our return, several of Epirotiki's ships were dockside at one time: the small *Neptune*, the mid-sized *Atlas*, the large *World Renaissance*, and our mid-sized ship, *Oceanos*. It was an impressive fleet, with most ships easily identified by their cream-colored hulls and white tops, and unique blue smokestacks sporting the insignia of a stylized gold Byzantine cross.

left: *Piraeus holds architectural gems on every day commercial streets as in this second floor balcony.*

146

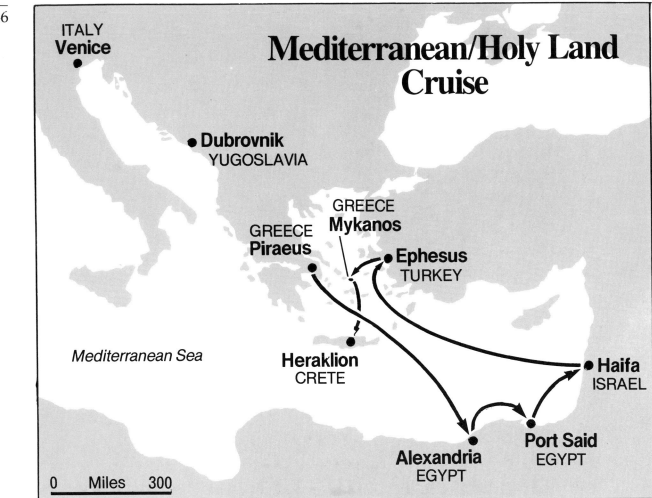

Mediterranean/Holy Land Cruise

ITALY
Venice

Dubrovnik
YUGOSLAVIA

GREECE
Mykanos

GREECE
Piraeus

Ephesus
TURKEY

Mediterranean Sea

Heraklion
CRETE

Haifa
ISRAEL

Port Said
EGYPT

Alexandria
EGYPT

0   Miles   300

Cruise ships in Greece offer so many varied itineraries that a visitor may return many times and sail to different islands.

To understand why so many of the ships were in port at one time, it's important to know of the variety of cruises offered by Epirotiki. The line offers Mediterranean trips lasting 1, 3, 4, 6, 14, or 20 days, from May to October. We were there in October.

Most package tours to Greece include a cruise segment. Itineraries from Athens vary in ports of call so that a visitor can return many times and sail to different islands. Our seven-day cruise was part of a fourteen-day Trans World Airlines Getaway package with three days in Athens before the cruise and a three-and-a-half-day motorcoach land trip following it. The itinerary included a stop on the island of Rhodes, the ports of Alexandria and Port Said, Egypt; Ashdod, Israel; the island of Patmos; Kusadasi, Turkey; and back to Piraeus. Optional shore excursions were available in each port.

Incidentally, this summer may be a bumper year for travel to Greece, as the exchange rate is favorable and tours take advantage of pre-booked fixed hotel rates along with air and shipboard costs. The biggest savings may be in cruises that include meals and entertainment.

Room with a view

On board the *Oceanos*, we were pleased with the layout of the ship, which has a large protected rear-deck space for enjoying the sun, the pool, and views of the sea and islands.

Cabins on the Epirotiki ships are attractive, as are the common rooms with themes from famous Greek legends and myths, rendered in strong, clear colors in plush wall decorations, statuary, mosaics, and paintings. Artist Arminio Lozzi and movie set designer Maurice Bailey collaborated on the decor.

The cabins were comfortable though not enormous. Ours had a double bed. Some have an extra fold-down berth to accommodate a third person at a reduced rate. Prices quoted for most packages include inside cabins on lower decks, with an added charge for a cabin with a porthole. We opted for the view.

Skeletal marble pillars on Rhodes still project the heroic images of ancient Greece.

Food with a Greek flair

The *Oceanos* specializes in Continental cuisine and features a wide variety of food with a definite Greek flair—which we enjoyed. Theme nights on board coordinate meals, entertainment, and dress—such as Greek Night, when we had Greek dishes, wore the flag colors of blue and white, and watched Greek entertainment.

In typical cruise fashion, there were numerous courses and generous servings at mealtime, starting with delicately flavored seafood appetizers, tasty soups, and salads generously heaped with late-season tomatoes, cucumbers, and Greek olives. Then came the entrees of native fish, lamb, beef, and pork, with a good variety of vegetables.

Happily, the dinner dessert choices were simple, usually with only one hugely rich dessert, a selection of ice cream, or fresh fruit and cheese. Conversely, a wide variety of temptingly rich desserts appeared on the lavish buffet table served on the upper deck at noontime.

Heading for shore

The excursions in each port were prearranged so that immediately after docking you could board a motorcoach for the destination. Some passengers on our cruise were disappointed, saying "the shore time was too short." For example, the time allowed on Rhodes was sufficient, except that a delay in leaving Athens meant a late arrival. And the excursion to Lindos on the other end of the island had to be rushed to get passengers back on time for the ship to sail. Later, at dinner, Captain Dionisios Papanikolatos explained that ships leave on time, because "we are charged for port time and fined heavily for late departures."

Outdoor, roof dining is a must—day or night.

IF YOU GO
Several cruise lines sail in the Mediterranean: Epirotiki, Sun Lines, Cycladic, K Lines, Royal Cruise Lines, and others. To book a Greek Islands cruise, contact your local travel agent or a firm specializing in cruises.

In some cases, as in Rhodes, taking an optional excursion away from the port eliminated any time for shopping. Mediterranean ports have lots of trinkets to sell, so, if shopping is a priority, don't sign up for the excursion.

Many languages on board

Oceanos provides two exceptionally well-trained Greek guides who give brief talks previewing the ports of call. "Vanna Theodoridou and I were trained at the National Tourist Organization School for tour guides at the University in Athens," said Anna Mellberg, who has sailed on cruise ships as a guide for five years. She continued, "I give the talks in Spanish and French, and Vanna gives the English, German, and Dutch. Between us we cover seven languages."

This is one of the pluses of Epirotiki cruises, since passengers come from all over the world. Our cruise had more people who spoke Dutch, German, Spanish, Portuguese, Greek, and Hebrew than ones who spoke English. We particularly enjoyed meeting and making an effort to communicate with non-English speakers at mealtimes, or on the sun deck. For excursions, passengers are assigned to motorcoaches by their language group.

Nightly entertainment

Until four years ago there was little entertainment aboard Epirotiki's ships. But now it has become part of each cruise. Sharron Emmins, the cruise director and a most attractive tall blonde who comes from Essex, England, introduced each show. "There are 15 entertainers on board. They're booked through a booking agency in London and shows are coordinated by our band director, Tony Christian," she said. "His combo, Tony Christian Sound, accompanies each show and plays for dancing," she added.

The nightly shows at 10:15 included a magic act, a delightfully funny clown act, a song and dance man from Scotland, two talented women vocalists; and a group of four energetic dancers. Although the level of sophistication in staging and costumes wasn't quite up to some glitzy shows on other cruise lines, most of the entertainment seemed to "work" all right for this part of the world.

What to wear?

There is a less formal dress code on Epirotiki's cruises than on some lines. "The longer cruises tend to have more formal occasions, shorter ones only first and last night out," said Emmins. My observation was that street length dresses for women and business suits for men were appropriate on formal nights.

Since Greece has a hot sunny climate, be sure to bring a sun hat, sunglasses, lotion, and cool clothing for shore trips. A plastic canteen for carrying water from the ship is handy since pure drinking water isn't easily found in this arid region. Some religious sites don't allow bare shoulders and shorts for women. Since most sites are usually high on a hill reached over well-worn and slightly slippery paths, good walking shoes are a must. A sweater is handy on deck most nights.

James Diedrick

STEAMING UP THE NORWEGIAN COAST: BREATHTAKING VISTAS, NATIVE CHARM

WE HAD DOCKED AT THE ISOLATED NORWEGIAN COASTAL VILLAGE of Berlevag, several hundred miles above the Arctic Circle and just around the corner from the Soviet border. There, a familiar ritual was being played out. Some 25 teenagers were standing on the pier in a state of great excitement. The ship's crane dipped down into the cargo hold and brought forth a bright fire-engine-red Honda motorcycle one of the group had bought. Before we set sail again, its new owner was doing figure eights in the parking lot to the delight of his friends—and of the tourists gazing down from the deck.

This was not an ordinary sea cruise. It was an 11-day, 1,500-mile round-trip journey from Bergen to Kirkenes on a 2,000-ton ship, one of 11 that leaves Bergen daily to take mail and cargo to thousands of isolated coastal residents.

Each coastal steamer is in fact a kind of hybrid, a cross between a tourist cruise ship and a cargo-carrying freighter. Tourist passengers can observe coverall-clad crew members loading crates of frozen fish and lumber one minute and be eating with sterling silver on china in the elegant dining room the next.

And although most of the tourists on board are English, German, and American, passengers are not isolated from the natives. Several dozen day-passengers are usually on board, most of them Norwegians using the ship to "bus" from one coastal county or town to the next.

left: *Our coastal steamer, the Ragnvald Jarl, in port at Honningsvag, the largest fishing village in West Finnmark.*

preceding pages: *The town of Nesna, where the local inhabitants gathered to greet the coastal steamer on May 17, Norwegian independence day. On May 17, celebrations take place all over Norway—dancing, singing, and dressing in traditional folk costumes.*

The city of Hammerfest is the world's northernmost town (exact latitude is 70 degrees 39 feet 48 inches latitude north). This view was taken from a trail up to Mount Salen. In the center, near the water, is the prominent landmark of St. Michael's Church.

This provides for many delightful encounters. On the fourth day of our journey, a Norwegian ornithologist came on board. He was studying the declining gannet and puffin populations above the Arctic Circle and spent most of his time with his binoculars and note pad. But he was always willing to talk about coastal customs and traditions.

One of the most persistent of these traditions involves a method of preserving cod, tons of which are caught in Norwegian coastal waters each year, especially between January and April. Beginning near the Lofoten Islands, some of the richest fishing grounds in the North Sea, a familiar sight greeted us on the jetties of the ports we called on: huge wooden A-frame structures, like tents that had lost their fabric. When we used our binoculars, we could see that hundreds of filleted fish were literally hanging out to dry on these racks.

This was, of course, an essential method of preservation in the days before refrigeration, and in fact many shippers made their fortunes by shipping what came to be called "clip-fish" to the Mediterranean—there to be consumed in Roman Catholic countries on fast days. A tradition born of necessity has become a cultural preference in Norway, where fish sellers do a brisk business in fish that have hung for months in the spring and summer air and must be soaked for days before they are edible.

The coastal steamers play an important role in this continuing commerce in fish, transporting a great deal of the processed cod, halibut, and salmon caught in the northern waters to Bergen, where it is loaded on to planes for destinations all over the world. We docked at Risoyhamn, in the Lofoten Island chain, for nearly two hours one morning and watched while 75 palettes (each containing about 20 cases of frozen cod fillets) were stowed in the ship's cargo hold.

Fortunately, not all of the fish is stored. One of the great attractions of the voyage is the opportunity it affords to sample the rich North Sea harvest of fresh cod, halibut, and salmon—not to mention a varied array of prepared fish, Scandinavian-style. In addition to eggs, porridge, bread, and preserves, the breakfast board was always loaded with several kinds of pickled herring, caviar in toothpaste-style tubes, and anchovies. Lunch spreads usually included shrimp, fish balls, and salt cod or herring.

Fresh fish was often featured at dinners as well. On the evening of National Day, May 17, when Norwegians celebrate their independence from Danish and Swedish rule, we were treated to a native feast: cauliflower soup, poached salmon with sour cream sauce, and new potatoes and carrots, followed by strawberries with cream and a bountiful array of flatbreads and cheeses.

Strolling on deck and eating are not the only activities for passengers. During the several stops the ship makes each day there are ample opportunities for sightseeing and shopping in the surprisingly varied coastal towns along the route. Several bus excursions are also arranged to provide an even closer look at coastal life.

Many of the larger towns boast one of the country's 41 "Husfliden" (home craft) shops, run by the Norwegian Association of Home Arts and Crafts. Their buyers select the best works from Norway's rural areas for display and sale— items such as hand-knit wool sweaters, scarves, and brightly painted wooden bowls and plates.

The towns in the southern half of Norway are lush with vegetation, as this area receives the full benefits of the Gulf Stream. But above the Arctic Circle, at the halfway point in the ship's journey north, the vegetation grows sparser. By the time the ship reaches the northeasterly towns of Vardo and Vadso, near Kirkenes, there are no trees to be seen.

There are compensations, though. Once past the Arctic Circle (and beginning about mid-May) the midnight sun begins to make its appearance, a spectral orb rising from its own embers to brighten the night sky with a pale, purifying light.

Even without trees, the scenery is consistently breathtaking. Sailing through the fjords is a little like cruising through a succession of flooded Yosemite valleys—a royal marriage of coastal water beauty and rugged alpine splendor.

Steaming up the Norwegian coast offers breathtaking vistas and native charm.

156

These waters have witnessed a great deal of important history, and not just during the Viking era. In April of 1940, Germany launched an attack on Norway and succeeded in occupying its major coastal ports as far north as Narvik, near the Lofoten Islands. The Germans then used these ports as staging grounds for their inland invasion.

For a short while during the war, Tromso, a coastal city north of Narvik, served as the capital of Free Norway and a center for resistance activities. In fact King Haakon and his government were headquartered here until they were forced to flee to England. And in 1944 British planes attacked and sank the German battleship *Tirpitz* near here after receiving information from Norwegian agents.

During the German invasion, many of the coastal towns were severely damaged by bombing raids, and when the Germans fled the Russians near the end of the war, they burned what was left to slow down their pursuers. Thus the architecture of a great many of the coastal towns is modern and uniform. Fortunately, such historic gems as the great cathedral at Trondheim were spared.

The coastal steamer makes two stops of several hours at Trondheim, affording visitors a tour of the cathedral, whose architecture echoes that of Westminster Abbey, but possesses a Gothic grandeur all its own.

Unfortunately, the days of this kind of coastal exploring may be numbered. The second officer of our ship said that the extension of roads and air landing strips into the northernmost coastal villages is jeopardizing the future of his ship and the 10 others like it. He predicted that within five years the steamers will no longer be making their year-round runs.

This would be a great shame. The splendor of the Norwegian coast will always remain, parts of it approachable by plane and car. But the experience of becoming a coastal voyager for 11 days can never be replaced.

Most visitors will want to spend several days in Bergen before or after the coastal voyage. A wide range of accommodations, from bed-and-breakfast hotels to private homes, is available. Write to the Bergen Tourist Board, Slottsgt. 1, 5000 Bergen, Norway, and ask for a Bergen Guide, which contains a comprehensive listing.

Both SAS and Northwest Orient fly to Scandinavia.

Islands in the Sun

Catalina—the Quaint
and the Untouched

Jamaica Offers More Than
Just Sand, Sea, and Seclusion

Victoria Would Have Loved
Hawaii's Royal Palace

Unique Vieques

Sanibel and Captiva:
Haven to
Beachgoers, Nature Buffs

Daniel B. Wood

CATALINA— THE QUAINT AND THE UNTOUCHED

"THERE'S OUR SAFEWAY GROCERY; THEY DELIVER. THERE'S OUR POST office; they don't," says the shuttle driver, Bob, on the 12 o'clock leg of Catalina Island's "Town of Avalon Tour."

He grinds gears on San Francisco-like hills, wrestles the steering wheel as the bus negotiates hairpin turns on one-way roads lined by palm and eucalyptus trees. Eventually, from a vantage point high above the small harbor, you look down at a square mile of whitewashed bungalows on stilts, Victorian bed-and-breakfast inns, and Spanish-style haciendas with glinting cobalt or burnt auburn roofs. This seaside southern California quaintness seems poured over the steep slopes of but one craggy cove of this otherwise untouched island.

Twenty-one miles long and anywhere from one-half to eight miles wide, Catalina is twice the size of Manhattan, but rugged, mountainous, and rustic. The only town, Avalon (pop. 2,200, with 800 registered cars), might fit on a single large city block. With no buildings more than a few stories high, the town is an architectural mix of rustic Spanish, brightly painted box cottages, and funky California ranch houses with highly individualized designs: tiling, skylights, gazebos, patios, porches, trellises, gates.

The rest of the island is a geologic monolith of scrubby coastal plants, cactuses, shrubs, and contorted hybrid oaks. Ironwood trees grow in the rocky cliff

left: *Catalina–the quaint and untouched.*

areas, which feature steep dropoffs to inaccessible pebble beaches. Hundreds of bison and thousands of goats, snakes, and foxes roam freely with, surprisingly, a large population of ravens overhead. Fourteen bison were brought to Catalina for co-starring roles in *The Vanishing American*, filmed here in 1924; they have since multipled to about 600. Other Hollywood films were made here, including *Mutiny on the Bounty* (1935), scenes from numerous Old West and South Sea movies, and the opening segment of the "Fantasy Island" television series.

Catalina has the most vegetation and wildlife of the eight channel islands— all formed by wrenching faults 25 million years ago. Eight plants are endemic and unique to the island—the Catalina cherry tree and St. Catherine's lace among them —and tour guides liken the island to the rest of southern California before development. Back in town, guides also play up what Avalon doesn't have: traffic lights, fast-food franchises, and portable stereos (the latter are illegal).

It was the Portuguese explorer Juan Rodriguez Cabrillo, sailing from Spain, who first claimed the island in 1542, naming it San Salvador. Sixty years later, another Spaniard named the island Santa Catalina for St. Catherine of Alexandria.

Chewing-gum magnate William Wrigley is credited with beginning Catalina's rise as a world-renowned playground. After purchasing the controlling interest in the Santa Catalina Island Company, which owned all the property in 1919, Wrigley invested huge sums of money to attract visitors. Projects included an enormous ballroom casino—the first round structure in southern California. There was also a bird park with "the largest birdcage in the world." Wrigley added thousands of extraordinary birds and invited the public, free. He also set up a baseball field, where his Chicago Cubs trained each spring. Catalina soon became a favorite vacation spot for stars in Hollywood's golden era, and not long thereafter became accessible to the public.

Today, construction on the island is severely restricted by the Santa Catalina Island Conservancy, which owns 86 percent of the island and seeks to preserve its natural wonder. Housing is so scarce that government-financed developments had to be built to accommodate government employees.

The number of daily cruise ships visiting Catalina from three mainland ports

Famous Avalon Casino contains a ballroom, theater, museum and art gallery.

—Long Beach, San Pedro, and Newport—has increased in recent years, according to the Chamber of Commerce. This reflects a general boom that saw the populace grow by one-third since the early 1970, along with a host of condominium projects, including a federal one offering low-income housing. Some of of these projects have left huge scars in the terrain. "For years, town planners have heralded a major master plan for the development of Catalina housing, but I've yet to see anything they say pan out," scoffs one 45-year resident.

Thirty hotels accommodate 3,000 visitors, many required to stay in three- or four-day intervals owing to the enormous demand that books the entire island for six-month seasons. Visitors must book hotels six months in advance, hotel owners say. The population on a given weekday is 5,000, and it's 10,000 on weekends during the summer, half that during winter. There are also 800 moorings and innumerable anchorings for yachting enthusiasts. A heliport and airport are handling more flights each season, but a seaplane service has been discontinued.

Once on shore, the short-time visitor has numerous attractions. Among these are the small harborside beach, tours of the town, island, and bay, and bicycles or golf carts to get around in. There is a riding stable and a nine-hole golf course. All types of restaurants abound, as do both serious and frivolous shops and clothing boutiques. Some are in commercialized arcades, which have an unfortunate sameness. Others are highly individualized, waiting around corners and down alleyways to be discovered spontaneously.

For the hiker, backpacker, and camper, Catalina is considered a paradise, though some have had run-ins with bison and all must make it to designated camping areas—Two Harbors or Blackjack Campsite recommended—before dark. Catalina is also considered one of the prime scuba and skin diving destinations in California, with clear waters, deep kelp beds, and aquatic life forms not seen elsewhere.

Debarking at 11:45 a.m. from the earliest two-hour voyage offered from Long Beach by Catalina Cruises, we signed up for three separate tours, which would nearly fill the time before the last cruise ship returned to the island at 4:30 p.m. We signed up for town and island tours and a glass-bottom boat tour of the harbor. All three move quickly and are full of information, professionally conveyed with lots of humor.

That left just a bit of time to walk the town, sample its stores, and rush back to the cruise ship. Besides restaurants, we missed one prime attraction, the 12-story Avalon Casino, built in 1929 by William Wrigley. Tours take you to the stately rotunda with an art gallery, museum, 1,200-seat theater, and a ballroom that used to swing to the sounds of Tommy Dorsey and Glenn Miller and where their modern counterparts carry on the tradition. But not seeing everything in one fell swoop keeps the interest piqued enough to begin planning return visits.

IF YOU GO

Santa Catalina Island is 25 miles off the coast of California near Los Angeles. Cruises to the island depart from downtown docks in Long Beach and San Pedro and take about two hours. Fares are $24.30 round trip for adults and $13 for children. Telephone (213) 514-3838 for exact locations and schedule. For more information on island activities, write to Santa Catalina Island, P.O. Box 217, Avalon, CA 90704, or call the Chamber of Commerce at (213) 510-1520.

Daniel B. Wood

JAMAICA OFFERS MORE THAN JUST SAND, SEA, AND SECLUSION

OUR MINIBUS FULL OF LUNCH-STARVED TOURISTS WAS BARRELING down that ribbon of hibiscus-lined highway from Montego Bay to Port Antonio when it happened.

Brushing a bank of sugar-cane stalks, we thwacked a chicken fluttering up from the undulating mirage of highway heat. With seconds to recover, we were now careening toward a stray cow and a broadly smiling Rastafarian with shoulder-length dreadlocks stuffed, as is common among that religious sect, beneath a colorful, wool-knit turban.

We missed the cow and the roadside Rastaman, who was holding a handful of tropical fruit for our perusal at 45 miles per hour. But the image of that tall, dark apparition, still smiling in the rearview mirror—part soul mate, part salesman, hospitable, ever expectant—is the image I still carry of Jamaica. Amid the wonderful rivers, falls, plantation "great houses," and gardens, it's the people—the human landscape—that stands out.

When it comes to highlighting the finer points of individual islands in the Caribbean, there's no use touting sand, sea, sun, scenery, and seclusion. So many islands have so much, that waxing poetic too often includes waxing generic.

On the other hand, the documented reason that 80 percent of all visitors come to the Caribbean is to flee northern winters. So if you're after the best of all

Crowds gather every day at Joe's in Negril Beach to cheer the sunset.

left: *Cliff diving into the naturally carved grotto at Negril Beach.*

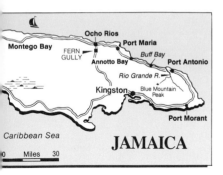

Jamaica's rich heritage includes
Arawak Indians, Spanish,
Africans and British.

worlds—an escape, a rich tapestry of culture, and wonderful people—which island should you choose?

Based on regular visits to more than 25 Caribbean islands during the past two years, I put my money on Jamaica. With a population of 2.2 million, Jamaica is larger, more literate, and has a more diverse economy than most of the Caribbean islands. Beyond the typical seclusion and water-based activities, it has the most diverse and accessible landscape, beaches, and natural attractions. From its rich heritage—Arawak Indian, Spanish, then British (until 1962)—it has a culture unique to the Caribbean, plus a variety of accommodations from which to enjoy it—from upscale to downright penurious, from lively to sequestered.

My accolades flow after overcoming a strong, built-in resistance to the island. Since 1980, Jamaica has pumped $8 million a year into television, radio, and print promotion. This has been largely aimed at turning around a negative image of the former regime of communist-leaning Prime Minister Michael Manley. Because of the public-relations blitz, Jamaica has probably the most commanding Caribbean profile in the American market.

Image-building efforts have included government-aided hotel refurbishings, and road, communication, and power improvements. Community groups have sprung up to promote their local tourist entities, and new laws have begun to standardize the quality of service, from luxury resorts to small pensions.

As a result, tourism has risen since 1980, surpassing bauxite as Jamaica's greatest earner of foreign exchange.

As for pure amenities, I can echo what Hugh Hart, minister of tourism and mining, told me: "Where else are there 7,000-foot mountains within a-half hour of the beach? Where else are there excellent trails through coffee and banana plantations past waterfalls and rivers? Where you can raft through the hinterland where no road possible could cross?"

Jamaica's socially conscious culture has produced not only reggae music, but also a unique cuisine that is consistently well prepared and reasonably priced from one end of the island to the other.

Most key sights are within a two-and-a-half-hour drive of each other. And they are different enough to make you feel you're on another island. You can't get too far away from theatrical presentations in the larger towns, or live reggae, the basis of a thriving recording industry. And the performing arts have developed to international levels with such acclaimed enterprises as the National Dance Theatre Company and the Jamaican Folk singers.

On one jaunt down the north shore, I was exhausted by the array of plantations with their wonderful, antique-filled "great houses," gardens, waterfalls, roadside artisan shops, caves, gorges. And these were merely side trips to augment staying in all manner of self-contained resorts. Guidebooks and travel agents can help you select from among the best in the Caribbean—among them Half Moon Bay in Montego Bay, and the Trident in Port Antonio. There the order of the day is relaxation: horseback riding, parasailing, sailboarding, swimming, fishing, and golf.

I have not been able to trim my list of "most memorable spots" to less than five:

• British playwright Sir Noel Coward's house, Firefly. High above Port Maria (where he lived, wrote, and painted until his death in 1973), Coward built this modest mountain retreat in 1956. With a melancholy view of the bay, it became a famous resting and congregating station to Broadway and Hollywood stars.

• Shaw Park Botanical Gardens, high above Ocho Rios. At 35 acres, this mountainside Eden is an impeccably manicured cornucopia of streams, ponds, views, and plants—bougainvillea, hibiscus, oleander, poinsettia.

• Prospect Plantation. On short tours here, you sample fresh-cut cane and watch a young native shimmy to the top of a palm tree for fresh coconut.

Native boat carved from log, awaits its owner for another day of bountiful fishing.

• Bamboo rafting down the Rio Grande. For nearly three hours, your boatman poles you through the rapids while singing wonderful calypso tunes and shaking ripe mangos from overhanging trees.

• Fern Gully, on the road from Ocho Rios to Kingston. Here is a lush, island rain forest where 700 species of fern thrive.

One of the island's disappointments for me was Dunn's River Falls, 600 feet of cascading fresh water that empties into the ocean. The drawback was not the stunning rock formations, but so much curio-hawking among the perimeter. It is smack-dab on the beaten tourist path near Ocho Rios and usually clogged with people.

Cuisine more than made up for the letdown. Morning meals include such delicacies as cold (or hot) banana porridge, salt cod and ackee (a red-skinned, yellow fruit resembling scrambled eggs), johnny cakes (fried flour dumplings), and plenty of tropical fruit. For lunch, restaurants offer all manner of spiced seafood, fried plaintain, squash, potato and pumpkin soups. On the street are wonderful spicy beef-filled pastries called "patties." Everywhere is "jerk chicken" and "jerk pork," spicy meats prepared in savory sauces, and cooked under corrugated zinc over smoking pimento wood.

Dinners feature fish, steak, chicken, crab, shrimp, and various kinds of soups and vegetables in African, Chinese, Indian, and European styles. Much of the cooking is hot and spicy—like Creole-or Cajun-style—and better prepared than anywhere else in the Caribbean.

Amenities aside, frequent reports of violence on the island leave tourists wondering if it's safe enough to visit. Jamaica has the highest police fatality rate in the world, but tourism officials say the problem is exaggerated and arises mostly in the capital of Kingston, away from the beaten tourist track of the north coast.

Many tourists never venture beyond their self-contained resorts, and they are thus largely shielded from the depressing shanty life that is the lot of far too many Jamaicans. It is West Kingston shanty villages with names like "Trench-town," "Lizard Town," and "Concrete Jungle" where the mean life that gave rise to reggae anthems still thrives. Tourists are advised not to venture there, but plenty of the curious do.

To help offset the dichotomy between the "haves" and the "have-nots," the government is trying to include all Jamaicans in the benefits of ever-increasing tourism. There are many local promotional campaigns to educate the populace on the value of unified hospitality to the outsider.

IF YOU GO

For information contact the Jamaica Tourist Board, 866 Second Ave., N.Y., NY 10017, (212) 688-7650.

left: *Conch shells cleaned and drying in the sun just steps from the water where they were retrieved.*

Ellen Steese

VICTORIA WOULD HAVE LOVED HAWAII'S ROYAL PALACE

ONE INTERESTING PLACE NOT TO MISS IF YOU'RE VISITING THE ISLAND of Oahu is the Iolani Palace.

It is the *only* royal palace on United States soil, as people here are fond of saying, a grand example of Victorian-tropical architecture. Its broad, Corinthian-columned façade looks immensely solid, almost indestructible.

And yet the world it was designed to showcase—a kingly life-style along the lines of European royalty—didn't last long. Thirteen years after the palace was built, the last queen of Hawaii was tried for treason here, in her own throne room.

Afterward, the palace became the capitol building for the new republic of Hawaii. The furnishings were auctioned; the huge carpet in the throne room was sold piece by piece; and termites attacked the great central koa wood staircase. Revolutions, even relatively peaceable ones, are unkind to kingly trappings.

But since 1969, when work began to restore the palace to its original state, millions of dollars have been spent, and today you can take a tour and imagine Iolani Palace in its brief but glorious heyday.

One of the guides — a group of gray-haired and fiercely protective haole ladies in Mother Hubbard dresses — will give you a pair of stretchy booties to put over your shoes. She'll then lead you through a door into the royal front hall.

You understand the booties after you enter. The hall, running from the front

Hawaiian motifs etched in the glass of the front door.

left: *Throne Room, where Hawaii's last queen was tried for treason.*

to the back of the building, has such an amazingly shiny floor that you can actually see a dim reflection of your face in it. The front door has Hawaiian motifs etched in glass and the center of the hall is dominated by a new and gleaming koa wood staircase.

Most interesting are the stately portraits of nine Hawaiian kings and queens that line the walls. But there's not much time to study them. Our guide is going over palace protocol, and has us, in our imaginations, dressed in silk and jewels, stepping from a carriage aided by a footman, and then sweeping through those etched glass doors into the Blue Room to wait for an audience with King Kalakaua.

The Iolani Palace was occupied by two rulers: King Kalakaua, a handsome man with Prince Albert side whiskers, who built the palace and gave himself a splendid coronation here, somewhat after the fact; and his sister and successor, Queen Liliuokalani.

There aren't many rooms in the entire building. Downstairs, there are only four. Behind the Blue Room is the dining room, whose table is set with crystal and silver, as for a banquet. Our guide showed us an elaborate breakfast menu — pigeons on toast, and ice cream among the many offerings — and explained that the Royal Hawaiian Band would have played out on the lanai as everyone ate.

Upstairs are four large, well-proportioned rooms full of sunshine. Here are found the king's bedroom and the queen's, the king's study lined with books, and a music room.

Curators had to go on a "treasure hunt" to find the pieces now in the palace. A visitor from Oklahoma City, looking at the photo of King Kalakaua's bedroom, recognized a small table in it as one in his own possession. A sharp-eyed palace curator spied a royal chair, encrusted with thick yellow enamel paint, in a thrift shop. One big wardrobelike piece was spotted in the local prison.

Next, our guide took us to a small room, a former guest room, where Queen Liliuokalani had been imprisoned. We heard the sad story of how the queen's government was overthrown in a brief and bloodless coup. While the queen waited for a reply to her appeal to the U.S. government to restore her rights, some of her supporters staged a counterrevolution, after which ammunition was found buried in the queen's own garden. The queen's trial was held downstairs, in the Throne Room, where she was found guilty of treason and sentenced to a $5,000 fine and five years of hard labor. The sentence was never carried out, but the queen did spend eight months imprisoned in the little second-floor room.

Our last stop was back down on the first floor in the Throne Room, handsome with its beautiful new rug—red with a sweeping design of ferns—a replica of the original. On either side of the two golden thrones at the far end were kahili, gorgeous feather-dusterlike objects that were symbols of Hawaiian roy-

right: Front hall of the Victorian–era Iolani Palace, restored and refurbished a decade ago; visitors must don soft booties to protect the gleaming floor and kao wood staircase.

alty before European-style palaces and coronations were ever thought of. Kahili warned the common people of a ruler's approach. Subjects were required to obey a strict code of behavior in the presence of royalty, with infringements punishable by death.

Generally, it seems that Victorian decoration won out over the Hawaiian in the palace. One feels that if Queen Victoria herself had owned an Hawaiian palace, it might have looked something like this. In fact, King Kalakaua had wanted to name his new home St. Alexander's Palace. But his advisers prevailed with the name Iolani, meaning "bird of heaven," the most sacred name in the Hawaiian language.

Old pictures of the palace, however, show attendants wearing feather capes and carrying huge kahili, indicating that in its day the place might have had a more Hawaiian look.

The kings of Hawaii are not forgotten. The Royal Hawaiian Band still plays outdoors on Fridays at 12:15, weather permitting; you can bring a bag lunch and sit on the lawn to listen. And a grand celebration still marks every royal birthday.

IF YOU GO

You need a reservation to visit the palace. Call (808) 523-0141, or write to Friends of Iolani Palace, Reservations, P.O.Box 2259, Honolulu, HI 96804. Cost is $4 for adults. The palace, located in Honolulu on Kings Street behind the state capitol, is open Wednesday through Saturday, from 9 a.m. to 2:15 p.m. For information call (808) 538-1471.

John Edward Young

UNIQUE VIEQUES

FOR ALL YOU FOLKS WHO WANT TO ADD SOMETHING NEW TO YOUR fried-dough repertoire—has Puerto Rico got a place for you! It's Vieques, a tiny island of about 8,000 people in the appropriate shape of a loaf of French bread, just off Puerto Rico's east coast. Here, during three days last November, in the sleepy, seedy, capital city of Isabel Segunda, everyone flocked to the central plaza for singing, dancing, cockfights, and throwing lighted matches across crowded sidewalks. It was all part of the first Festival Arepas. It was clear from the start that it would become an annual affair.

Small stalls and kitchenettes-on-wheels sold *arepas*, a hot, rather tasteless and greasy, local fried dough that is a staple in every kitchen here. During the festival, tons of the coaster-size pieces of bread were eagerly consumed by skateboarders, strollers, grandmothers, American Navy servicemen, and tots alike. Local soft drinks work as well as dishwashing detergent to help dissolve the fat and wash these sinkers down. Be warned about one drink canned under the catchy non sequitur "Kola Champagne India." The pink, bubble-gum-flavored carbonated beverage does not help a mouthful of fried dough go down.

Between the many spirited festivals and holidays held here, things don't just quiet down; they virtually come to a screeching halt. There's little in the way of entertainment in the capital city, apart from a bit of shopping at the local video

left: *Vieques boasts true beauty on its 40 uncrowded, palm-trimmed beaches.*

174

Vieques is a tiny island shaped like a loaf of French bread with about 8,000 inhabitants.

store, wig shop, supermarket, or at Central Comercial, where you may find everything in the way of bicycle, scuba gear, and hamster-care needs.

If you do find yourself in Isabel Segunda around lunchtime, stop in at the Green Palace Pizza, or, better yet, stop in for a bowl of chili or a fish dish at La Cueva. The latter is a small restaurant off the city square run by an expatriate New York policeman named Bob. "I used to run a bar in the States," he says. "But I got sick of breaking up fights." There's little to worry Bob here. Even in the controlled frenzy of an *arepas* festival, the locals are pleasant and well behaved.

With the exception of Fort Isabel Segunda—a 19th-century brick structure that crowns the city, and a sprinkling of pretty villas, Vieques's true beauty lies outside the city limits—mostly along its 40 uncrowded, palm-trimmed beaches.

A 20-minute drive from Isabel Segunda on a paved road lined with hedges of red hibiscus is Esperanza Beach Club and Marina. Once the center of the sugar industry, this area is now given over to fishers of snapper, conch, grouper, crab, lobster, and octopus.

The tiny island off shore is a perfect stop for snorkeling or reef diving. You'll find nine-foot-long leopard rays out there, and a few puffer fish among the striped butterfly fish and colorful wrasse. "Just don't touch the tail of the ray," we were warned as one "flew" off 20 feet below us.

Certainly the most interesting lodging on the island is a half-mile from Esperanza at La Casa del Frances. The Great House of this former plantation was built around the turn of the century. The formal, white two-story building, with its central atrium, is filled with Haitian art and Terry Price sculptures. A certain Tennessee Williams kind of steamy elegance prevails. It's now run by a colorful, delightfully eccentric ex-Bostonian, Irving Greenblatt. (Eccentric Bostonian, I was told by one of our group, was redundant. An obvious dig at *my* hometown —and a remark I did my best to grin and ignore!)

"This is the only hotel in the world where people don't steal the towels," Dr. Greenblatt said as he gave an informal tour of the place. "They're too thin and scratchy. In fact, people send us towels. The bed linens don't match, either. And if anyone complains, they get the Miss Piggy sheets," he added, milking the twinkle in his eye. Everything is laid back and informal. "We put people to work, too," says cook Jim Arnett. "If guests come into the kitchen looking bored, we'll have them prepare and serve the hors d'oeuvres. And if anyone wants a peanut butter sandwich during the day, they just come in and help themselves."

No matter how you fill your days on Vieques —fishing, swimming, tracking wild horses, or chasing mongooses—don't leave without a swim in glowing Mosquito Bay on a dark and preferably moonless night. (Actually the name Mosquito bugged the local government, hence its new, more appropriate name —Phosphorescent Bay.)

A dive into this inky water agitates microscopic *dinoflagellat*es organisms, which give off a cold, luminescent light. The whole effect has been variously described as like swimming in champagne or nuclear waste! However you see it, the experience is great fun and exhilarating: a bit like playing Tinkerbell underwater, or the swimming pool scene in the movie *Cocoon*.

The night life here is pretty much confined to the cockroach population; so if you prefer a more active after dark scene, it's best to stay in San Juan, on the main island. There are no high-rise hotels or casinos, and, if there is a disco in town, I missed it.

But if you want to get away from traffic, noise, and city life, and stop—or at least slow down —Vieques may be just the place you're looking for.

IF YOU GO

There's little more you'll need in Vieques than a bathing suit, towel, an appetite for *arepas*, and a can of industrial-strength mosquito repellent. If you wish to stay at La Casa del Frances, you must book well in advance. Dr. Greenblatt may accept you, and then, again, he may not. Write him a nice letter at P.O. Box 458, Vieques Island, PR 00765. There's a 10-day minimum in season; rates start at about $60. It's not quite as much fun but certainly easier to get a room at Esperanza Beach Club & Marina, P.O. Box 1569, Vieques Island, PR 00765. For details contact Puerto Rico Tourism Co., 575 Fifth Ave., New York, NY 10017, or call (212) 599-6262.

There's little more you'll need on Vieques than a bathing suit, towel, and an appetite for arepas.

Hilary DeVries

SANIBEL AND CAPTIVA: HEAVEN TO BEACHGOERS, NATURE BUFFS

IT TELLS YOU A LOT ABOUT A PLACE WHEN THE MAIN HEADLINE IN the local paper reads, "Loggerhead turtles wash ashore." The week before it was updates about baby egrets returning to their nests. So goes the breaking news on Captiva, part of a 25-mile-long brace of islands dangling off the west coast of Florida, which conchologists have christened one of the three best shelling beaches in the world.

It's a safari's worth of wildlife crammed into a space about the size of Manhattan Island. More than 300 species of fauna punctuate the area. It's the kind of wilderness that has appealed to outdoorsmen and environmentalists—Teddy Roosevelt and Anne Morrow Lindbergh, as well as scores of tourists—for more than five decades. Before that, the islands drew the likes of Ponce de León, along with Gasparilla and a smattering of other seagoing pirates, who named the one spit of land for their female captives (Captiva) and the other (Sanibel) for Isabella, Queen of Spain.

And then, of course, there are the shells. And more shells. So many, in fact, that residents speak of the "Sanibel stoop" when referring to beachcombers who move about with the posture and intensity of dowsers. That's what more than 300 types of seashells and a particular confluence of tides, trade winds, and geography will get you.

Sanibel and Captiva have been a haven to beachgoers and nature buffs from as early as 1521.

left: *Over 300 species of birds attract both environmentalists and outdoorsmen alike.*

178

Florida's Sanibel and Captiva islands are a safari of wildlife sights crammed into the size of Manhattan.

Out-of-towners have been coming to Sanibel ever since 1521, when Diego Marvilo sailed up the coast and discovered that Florida was not an island. Before 1963, the absence of any access except by ferryboat kept mainlanders to a minimum. Since then a two-lane toll causeway has increased the number of tourists. In 1974, the islands locked horns with nearby Fort Myers and came away with civic autonomy. A subsequent city charter sharply curtailed commercial development, and the islands' conservative land-use plan is considered something of a landmark.

Not only has the limited condominium and hotel construction retained the islands' semi-exclusivity; it has also preserved much of the original environment. This is Olde World Florida, where the whelks and coquinas roam and the alligators and egrets play right alongside you on the local golf courses.

For the hard-core preservationist, a visit to the Ding Darling National Wildlife Refuge is a must. This 5,000-acre preserve, administered by the U.S. Department of the Interior, includes mangrove swamps, pine forests, and wetlands occupying nearly the entire northwest half of Sanibel. Established in 1945, the refuge—which is laced with walking, driving, and canoe trails for easy access—honors the late Ding Darling, founder of the National Wildlife Federation and a nationally syndicated conservation cartoonist. Found within the refuge's leafy confines are nearly 300 bird species. It is possible to spot rare roseate spoonbills, wood ibises, and bald eagles, along with the occasional Atlantic loggerhead turtle and American alligator.

Lest the potential vacationer think the islands fit terrain for only hardy nature stalkers, however, Sanibel and Captiva do offer more Sybaritic pursuits. If one's pleasures run to boardsailing, jet skiing, sailboating, or driving "topless" cars, local rental businesses can fill the bill. For more run-of-the-mill activities, the islands offer tennis, golf, swimming, and beachgoing in abundance. Nearly every hotel and condominium complex has at least one pool, a couple of tennis courts, and good beach access. The new Sonesta Sanibel Harbor Resort, perched at the end of the causeway, boasts 12 outdoor courts open to the public as well as a center court, the site of the annual PaineWebber Classic tennis tournament.

Sanibel offers two public golf courses, though not of championship quality. One of them, the Dunes, has 18 holes. South Seas Plantation, on the tip of Captiva, the toniest resort on the islands, has its own private nine-hole course. In fact, everything about the 330-acre resort is private except for one of its restaurants, Chadwick's, and a local branch of the Off-Shore Sailing School.

By and large, the majority of island vacationers stay in rented condominiums. The islands appeal to families and long-term visitors, and the self-contained, apartment-style units are popular, with condo complexes vastly outnumbering hotels. Four island agencies handle most of the accommodation transactions. These include Executive Services Inc., Priscilla Murphy Real Estate, John Naumann Associates Inc., and a local branch of Merrill Lynch. A spacious three-bedroom condo on Captiva starts at $1,350 a week in high season (January-April), while a one-bedroom on Sanibel starts at $850. Room rates at two island hotels, Song of the Sea on Sanibel and 'Tween Waters Inn on Captiva, run to the $140-a-night range in peak seasons. Both offer efficiency accommodations. There is also one RV park and campsite on the island—Periwinkle Park and Campground. It tends to get booked up early.

While mainland tourist attractions in nearby Fort Myers and Naples may initially lure the visitor—a walk through the winter home of Thomas Edison is particularly worthwhile—everyone sooner or later settles down to an island lifestyle, the three-mile causeway notwithstanding.

Conchologists have christened Captiva, one of a 25–mile long brace of islands, one of the best shelling beaches in the world.

180

IF YOU GO

Like the rest of Florida, the islands tend to get booked during peak season—January to April—so call ahead and reserve accommodations: Chamber of Commerce, (813) 472-1080; Priscilla Murphy, (813) 472-4113; John Naumann Associates Inc., (800) 237-6004; Executive Services Inc., (800) 237-6002. Most major carriers, fly in and out of Fort Myers's airport. It's advisable to rent a car either at the airport or on the island.

Although upscale, the islands are not as self-consciously exclusive as Palm Beach or even Naples. There is a vacation-home feel to the place, and bare feet and shorts are the usual attire. A stable year-round population helps keep things in balance as well. On the beach, retirees in sun hats and children with sand pails comb the beach alongside the string-bikini set.

Indeed, the most frequent "occupation" on these shell-washed islands is beachgoing. Sanibel's famous Spring Shell Fair is held every March, and pamphlets on the how-to's of shelling are found everywhere. At local shell shops one can round out a collection with extra-large horse conchs and hunks of rare red or purple coral.

Other favorite pursuits of this frequent visitor include browsing in the MacIntosh Book Shop, visiting the Schoolhouse Gallery, and breakfasting with an armload of newspapers at the 'Tween Waters Inn dining room. That is when I can't be found on the narrow, palm-shaded beach within arm's reach of the Mucky Duck, Captiva's most popular—and only—beachside café. Those in search of culture, popular and otherwise, can visit the lone movie theater or the island's historic theater, Pirate Playhouse. Otherwise, try reading the papers and catching up on the wildlife news.

Don't feed the gorilla

One island must see is the famous Bubble Room Restaurant on Captiva. This low-slung pink stucco site with a palm tree growing through the roof brings to mind a hideaway for the seven dwarfs rather than any credible eatery.

Since its 1978 founding by Jamie Farquarson, a San Antonio handbag designer, it has become an island staple. Famous out-of-towners (Willard Scott) and locals (Bob Phillips, the voice of Porky Pig) regularly stop by for heaping plates of ribs, chicken, beef, and the mountainous desserts homemade by Farquarson's wife. Waitresses and waiters are dressed in khaki shorts and merit badges and blithely refer to themselves as "Bubble Scouts."

Decor is early Santa's Village and clearly the main attraction. The hour's wait for your table—no reservations—can be whiled away carefully inspecting the wind-up dolls, marionettes, and Christmas tree lights, including the simmering bubble lights for which the restaurant is named.

The piano player on the third floor tickles the ivories next to an all-but-life-size stuffed camel. A whistling model train runs throughout the restaurant on an overhead track. During your meal, Farquarson propels a wooden alligator across patrons' feet.

"Careful, he bites," he cautions. Outside, a sign in an empty animal cage reads, "Do Not Feed Bo Bo Bubble The Gorilla. He May Go Ape And Escape." Tourists should not.

Back to Africa

Tough But Amazing:
That's the Tassili

On Safari
to Glimpse Elusive
Mountain Gorillas

Senegal's Door of No Return

Serendipity Safari

Julia Wakefield

TOUGH BUT AMAZING: THAT'S THE TASSILI

THE ROCK PAINTINGS IN THE MIDDLE OF THE SAHARA SOUNDED unusual. I wanted to go see them, but it's a good thing I planned ahead. It took four months to organize a vacation to the Tassili N'Ajjer (the Plateau of Rivers), in Southern Algeria.

Letters to the American and Algerian embassies and the Algerian travel agency went unanswered.

With only days left before my scheduled departure, a letter from the American Embassy's cultural attaché came to the rescue. This office arranged for transportation into Algiers, made hotel reservations, and arranged for me to join a group going to see the paintings.

The tour included three days in the sprawling capital city of Algiers along the Mediterranean. Algeria isn't an especially easy place for an American to be a tourist. It's a totally French-speaking country, and it's expensive. Outside Algiers, there are not many restaurants. Among the few hotels for tourists in the city are the Hotel D'Jazair, a restored Turkish palace, and the Hotel Suisse, where you can't count on having running water 24 hours a day.

On the day we left the city to see the rock paintings, we needed to be at the airport at 5 a.m. The two-hour, 1,000-mile flight from Algiers south to Djanet, lands at a military airport, 30 kilometers from the Arab village of Djanet.

Brassware maker in the Casbah, Algiers.

left: *Visiting along the streets of Djanet.*

184

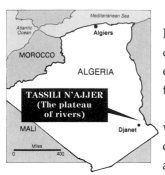

Algeria, pinpointing Tassili N'Ajjer.

Women carrying laundry home from central water source in Djanet.

The village is nestled in a narrow valley between the Tassili Plateau and the lava hills, at the edge of the desert. The streets in Djanet are lined with tall, thin, dark-skinned men, dressed in long, loose robes, called *gondurahs*, and turbans in either white, black, or drab green, called *sheshes*. Late in the day, when the temperature drops, a few veiled women appear.

The hub of activity is the Hotel Zeribas, which consists of 40 grass huts, each with two sagging beds, a lopsided table, and a dangling bare light bulb. An oversized skeleton key opens your own door, as well as any of the others. Meals are served in a warehouselike building. There's also a shaded patio bar, where music blares. A night at the Hotel Zeribas costs $30, including meals.

The market, with its orange tangerines and red tomatoes, is a great place to take pictures of locals bargaining for brightly colored material or shoes made from used tires.

Two different trips to the paintings can be arranged through the local tour agency, called Timbeur.

One is a day tour to Jabbaren, which means "the Giants," because the paintings found there are of giant, round-headed monsters with massive legs and tattooed bodies. Some figures carry basket-shaped vessels on their heads. Others look like men from outer space.

The other offering is a five-day guided tour, with burros carrying all gear. It's necessary to hire a guide for either tour, as it's impossible to find your own way to the paintings or back.

On the drive to the trailhead, you'll pass long, strange shadow figures on the golden sand, as the sun rises behind cross-hatched rocky spires typical of the extra-terrestrial look of the Tassili. After a short, steep climb on foot up a gorge choked with house-sized rocks, you arrive on the Tassili Plateau. Your guide will show you about 20 panels of rock art each day, which are actually not many, when you realize that there are over 5,000 panels in the Jabbaren area alone, all dating back to 4000 B.C.

The experience of staying overnight in the Tassili and sleeping under the stars on hard sand will stay with you a lifetime. The quiet is almost deafening. There's not even the intrusion of an airplane, as in the southwestern deserts of the United States. No crickets sound; no frogs croak.

It's hard to comprehend the ochre paintings on the sandstone walls and under rock overhangs. They depict graceful, running warriors carrying bows and arrows, or campfire scenes.

Along with arrowheads, knives, and scrapers, the paintings are all that remain of an unknown civilization. They are proof that what we know as the barren Sahara was once a savannah inhabited by a civilization supporting large herds of cattle, as well as giraffes, elephants, and hippos.

After seeing the paintings, you'll wonder how anyone ever found them, for some are hidden under overhangs lower than table height.

The mysteries of the Tassili art will continue to intrigue you long after you return home.

IF YOU GO

The Timbeur agency is the only tour agency in Djanet (mailing address is simply Djanet, Algeria) and it's very efficient and well-organized. You can book a Tassili rock art tour stateside through a local travel agent or the Adventure Center, 5540 College Ave., Oakland, CA 94618. Call (outside CA) (800) 227-8747 or (in CA) (800) 228-8747. Several airlines, including Air France and Lufthansa, serve Algiers. The best months for visiting the interior of Algeria are May, June, and October. Book your Algiers-to-Djanet flight on Air Algérie *before* you leave the U.S.; to do so in Algiers takes at least half a day. There are two flights weekly. You'll also need visas for Algeria and for France, if you change planes there. Bring a canteen and iodine tablets for purifying water in the desert.

On the Tassili Plateau guides proudly show drawings dating back to 4000 B.C.

Linda L. Liscom

ON SAFARI
TO GLIMPSE
ELUSIVE MOUNTAIN
GORILLAS

THE JUNGLE IS DENSE, THE TERRAIN STEEP, AND AT 8,000 FEET THE AIR thin. Sylvester swings a machete through pillared vegetation, and I follow, trudging through hanging vines and stinging nettles, pulling myself up the mountain on bamboo handholds. Underbrush and downed timber make footing unstable, and when my boots touch the ground, they're sucked deep into the mud. It's too high for snakes, but worms the size of frankfurters take their place.

Despite a powerful body, the gorilla has delicate manners.

We're tracking mountain gorillas in the lush jungles of Rwanda's Virunga Volcanoes, where about 250 of these noble, gentle beasts remain alive in their struggle against extinction.

Four groups of gorillas have been habituated to human visitors. Each group, *if* it can be found, can be visited for one hour once a day by up to six guests, under the strict supervision of trained guides. Although the gorilla permit doesn't guarantee gorillas, guides know their whereabouts from the previous day. There's no trail, and the search can last from half an hour to four hours before being abandoned.

On our visiting day, we meet our guides, Sylvester and Francisco, stately young black men outfitted in green berets, camouflage suits, and shoulder-slung rifles. They explicitly outline behavior protocol — in French:

left: *As guests in the home of the mountain gorilla our presence alone is a threat to poachers.*

Rwanda with Virunga National Park.

• No talking, no pointing, no eye contact; crouch when the guide crouches. Stature and eye contact are considered threats by the gorillas.

• If infants touch you, don't touch back — move slowly away.

• If the silverback charges, crouch and remain silent — never run or scream. (The silverback is the 350-pound dominant group leader, whose name derives from a saddle of gray hair that develops across the back of 12-year-old males when they reach full maturity.)

An hour of arduous climbing brings us to the nesting site where the gorillas spent the previous night — foot and knuckle imprints and fresh droppings still visible. Not far ahead we hear thrashing, the cracking of limbs, and a low, throaty noise resembling an operatic bass clearing his throat. The gorillas! Our guides imitate their vocalizations of contentment and continue the vocal exchange throughout our hour-long visit with the group.

We crouch on a steep slope just short of the silverback, which is climbing a cluster of bamboo trees above us. He situates himself on the arbor throne, dismisses us with an acknowledging glance, and gets to the prime order of business: lunch. Despite his powerful body, he has delicate manners. He plucks one tender leaf at a time from a branch and divides each one into several mouthfuls, as we would savor a delicious cookie — one bite at a time.

Meanwhile, in another clump of trees, a female free-falls 20 feet before grabbing a branch. One mother gives climbing lessons while another gives her offspring lunch-gathering lessons, extending the little one's reach with piggyback support. A three-year-old settles into a noon meal of tender, peeled wild celery and succulent thistle stems.

Close observation of these dignified creatures is an incomparable experience. As guests in the home of the mountain gorilla, we are one of the keys to conservation strategy. Our presence alone is a threat to poachers — and tariffs from permits help provide the funds needed for the national park to enforce antipoaching rules. Permit fees also support local education programs aimed at preserving the small gorilla habitat, which has been shrinking as farmland spreads.

Rwanda's Mountain Gorilla Project (MGP), the organization protecting the mountain gorilla, is proud of this statistic: no poaching in 1984 or 1985. Before its formation in 1979, as many as 15 gorillas were killed annually. Recently, mountain gorilla populations have not only stabilized but have seen the percentage of young gorillas increasing. Thanks to technical and financial assistance from international organizations, including the World Wildlife Fund, MGP has recently launched projects in Zaire and Uganda.

It has been a desperate fight. Poachers are after trophies, or young gorillas captured for sale to zoos. To capture the infant may mean destroying every adult in the group, as gorillas will fight to the death to defend their young. And the final blow: Mountain gorillas do not survive in captivity.

Louis Leakey early realized that the mountain gorilla could be doomed to extinction in the same century in which it had been discovered. Between 1960 and 1966, following the first study of the mountain gorilla in the wild by George Schaller, the population halved. For the next 15 years, Dian Fossey lived among the gorillas and conducted long-term field studies. She lived and died for the mountain gorilla. They lost their closest friend when Dr. Fossey was murdered, presumably by poachers, in her park cabin.

My experience in the home of the mountain gorilla left me in speechless ecstasy. And as we descended the mountain, I remembered something Fossey wrote in her book, *Gorillas in the Mist*. It was a quotation by Jody from *The Yearling* — ``I done seen me something special today.''

A Rwanda mountain gorilla expedition, including two days of gorilla tracking, requires five days and may be arranged as an extension for a Kenyan, Tanzanian, or other African safari. Animal lovers of all ages in good physical condition can make the trip. Be sure to take rain gear and warm clothes. Annual rainfall in the Virungas is 70+ inches, accompanied by chilling fogs.

Our guide imitates the gorilla vocalizations of contentment throughout our visit.

Bunny McBride

SENEGAL'S DOOR OF NO RETURN

AT THE END OF A DARK STONE CORRIDOR IN GOREE ISLAND'S HOUSE of Slaves lurks a rectangular hole filled with the blazing light of sun reflected from the Atlantic. It is known as the "Door of No Return." Through this portal, millions of blacks were wrenched from their homeland to build the civilizations of strangers in faraway worlds. Nearly 20 percent died before they could be delivered to markets in the Americas.

Situated at the westernmost tip of Africa, Gorée was the closest and most vital slave trade depot to America. It is said to be the last piece of home viewed by half of some 10 million Africans shipped across the Atlantic between the 15th and 19th centuries. The island lies cradled in the lee of Cap Verdi Peninsula, three kilometers (about two miles) from Senegal's coastside capital, Dakar, which vies with the Ivory Coast's Abidjan for the nickname "Paris of West Africa."

In 1977, Alex Haley made the region notorious in the United States through a television production of his book *Roots*, which chronicles the history of a black American family beginning with its West African ancestors. Before *Roots*, most tourists who ventured to Dakar came from France. They pursued the former French colony for seaside sun and an opportunity to glimpse at African exotica from a base of city comfort such as the elegant Teranga Hotel. Although French visitors still outnumber all others here, Americans now flock to the area. Some

Through this door
For a voyage without return
They would go, their eyes fixed
On the infinity of their suffering.

Joseph Ndiaye
Maison des Esclaves

30,000 went last year—nearly one-sixth of the total tourist count.

New arrivals spend their days basking on lovely city-side beaches and gadding among the brilliant flowers and fabrics of Dakar's bustling Kermel and Sandaga markets. They dine on savory French cuisine in restaurants that overlook a sunlit or moonlit sea. Despite such city delights, if you talk with people after a stay in Dakar, they are apt to mention Gorée Island first. The island's simple beauty, in contrast with its miserable history, makes it a haunting place not easily forgotten.

I ventured to Gorée from Dakar on the *Biasie Diagne*, a rotund white ferry named for the first African member of the French National Assembly. To find a seat, passengers must climb over bundles of fresh-cut flowers, boxes of vegetables, and crates of fish —supplies for Gorée's only restaurant, the Chevalier de Boufflers. (There is no locally grown food on the island, whose 1,000 inhabitants survive through tourist trade, crafts, and fishing.)

As we nose away from the loading docks, cranes, cargo ships, and oil silos of Dakar's harbor, I can see Gorée before us, its faded rose-hued buildings sunstruck atop black volcanic rock in a gray-blue sea. As we dock, teenage boys, self-appointed guides, approach passengers in a friendly, unpushy manner. One boy points me toward the House of Slaves. All around me, there is the silence of no cars. Courtyards bloom with bougainvillea, and lines of colorful laundry sway in the breeze. Until I reach my destination, the serenity of this 88-acre world fully belies its history.

With other visitors, I step through the arched entryway of the House of Slaves into a dirt courtyard burning with noontime sunlight. Here we meet Joseph Ndiaye, a serious but enthusiastic man who has been custodian of the building since it was established as a museum 17 years ago. Ndiaye was born on Gorée in the days when it was a home for a series of local families or a shop for selling drinks. But even then, Ndiaye was digging into the history and telling people about it. "My vocation was to be something in this place," he says. "To bring out its meaning, to help people be sensitive to what happened here."

Ndiaye leads us across the courtyard, down a small set of steps, and into the dark, narrow corridor that weaves between sinister dungeons. We pass a poster noting the dates slavery was abolished in various corners of the world: "Chile 1780 . . . United States 1863 . . . Mauritania 1981." We peer into the confines of a 7-by-8-foot room that was a cell for 20 men. Corroded metal fittings that once held chains cling to the walls. We move on to a longer but narrower chamber where children were kept, then past a hall leading to the Door of No Return. Next, a tiny, shoulder-high cubicle for "recalcitrants." And a room for virgins. Visitors are timid about stepping into the dank cells, as if fearing the heavy doors will close behind them.

We recross the courtyard to the large Weight Room, where Dutch, French, British, and American slave traders examined and weighed their human cargo. It is another world up those stairs. Spacious chambers. Smooth wooden floors. Huge windows that call in sunlight and sea breeze. Doors that are 11 feet high and open onto balconies overlooking Dakar. There is an art exhibit here now — the work of a Guatemalan man who lives on Gorée. The paintings are a haunting mix of grace and pathos — blurry black figures floating among sprays of pink and blue pastel.

Coming down from the merchants' airy quarters, I walk toward the Door of No Return. Standing at the gateway, I imagine a woebegone stream of black men, women, and children passing through the door into a floating prison on a pale sea. Here on this island, named Gorée by Dutch slavers in the 17th century, I sense history in a way I've never felt in Amsterdam, Paris, or London. I'm struck by the fact that up through this very day there is a tragic flaw in what we call *progress*: Too often it happens for one group of people at the cost of another.

Go to Gorée. It is bound to stir the genuine fellowship within each of us.

> ### IF YOU GO
> Several airlines fly to Dakar; Sabena, SwissAir, Air Afrique, and Pan Am with connections to Europe. From Dakar one takes a bus to Cape Almadies and a ferry to Gorée Island. For more information call your travel agent.

Gorée, the western most tip of Africa, was the closest distance to America on the tragic slave route.

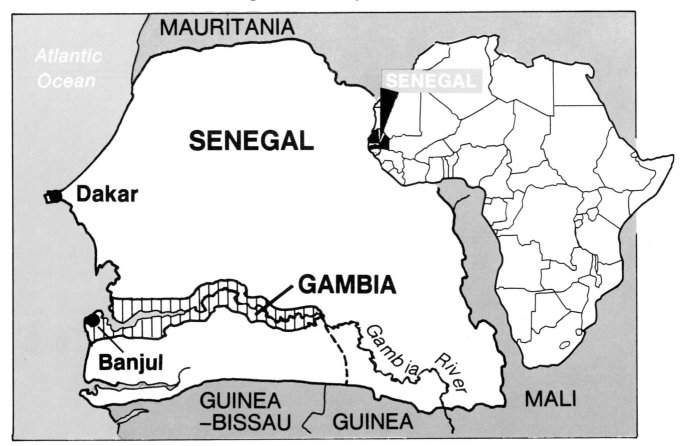

Nancy Herndon

SERENDIPITY SAFARI

ONE HUNDRED MILES BETWEEN THE TRAFFIC JAMS OF MODERN NAIROBI and the nearest game reserve, Masai Mara, the giraffes browse at will—cautious, alert, at home in the brown-and-gold oven of the Great Rift valley.

We left Nairobi on a safari of our own making with a station wagon rented for $400 a week, two good maps, a guidebook, camping equipment, and a rough itinerary that includes the game reserves of Masai Mara, Lake Naivasha, and Amboseli.

Now, hours from our first destination, our foursome stops at a desolate crossroad. Beside a bridge, multicolored longhorned cattle wade neck-deep in brown water. A Land Rover roars past us, and we speed past a slim-legged boy driving a donkey, to arrive in the town of Narok, with its three gasoline stations, Barclay's Bank, two-story restaurants with the scent of grilled meat, and corrugated iron sheds selling Masai jewelry.

The pavement ends, and our pace slows to a jolting crawl. Pale dust rises around the car and sifts down the windshield. In the rugged landscape, flat-roofed villages of mud and brush blend organically in the gray rocks. A church mission, its bright grass and flowers attesting to the presence of a modern irrigation pump, seems as remote as a falling star.

Then we see the gates of Masai Mara National Reserve, and in a moment we

Young male lion keeps his keen eye on the 700 square miles of undeveloped wilderness of Masai Mara.

left: *Elephants freely roam the Kenyan game reserves.*

Lioness in early morning looks for a meal.

are paying park fees ($5 a person per day) to a uniformed officer who speaks in clipped English. In this unlikely geography, we arrive at one of the most luxurious vacation spots on earth.

The Masai Mara covers 700 square miles of largely undeveloped wilderness. Its attraction is that it is an extension of Tanzania's Serengeti Plain, where 2 million wildebeests, zebras, and gazelles circle in annual migration, concentrated in the Mara from August to October.

In January, when we visit, the herds are smaller, a hundred or so animals together, but all the common species are present. As we bump down the reserve's graded road, wildebeests snort and stamp with anger, kick up their heels, and flee. Delicate-boned duikers romp, rearing and locking horns in play. Massive African buffalo watch us intently, standing their ground or walking aggressively toward our car. At a water hole a giraffe bends its awkward legs to drink.

A swarm of safari vans, pop-up tops open for cameras and video lenses, converge by a herd of Thomson's gazelles, that scatter out across the landscape, and converge again by a den of hyena pups.

Operated by organized tours and safari lodges (for $20 a day per person), the network of safari vans is a ubiquitous species wherever visitors are allowed. Dependable and quick, but totally without safari mystique, the vans "track" rarer species with CB radios; a leopard spotted by one van is news throughout the reserve within minutes.

After several days of sighting animals at random, we ask the driver of a safari van to "track" a cheetah for us. He sends out the call and gets our directions: Look under the third big tree after you turn left at the airstrip. Sure enough, two drowsy cheetahs, eyes half-closed, lounge under that tree. Ernest Hemingway never had it so easy.

But the reserves no longer permit his brand of adventure. Game hunting is outlawed, and bush camping is restricted to areas near safari lodges. In the camping area ($1.50 a person) behind Keekorok Lodge, a herd of zebras grazes beside an old campfire, moving shyly away into the bush as we approach.

The lodge itself is the stuff of dreams. "Tent" accommodations, complete with carpeting, hot showers, and electricity, go for $100-$150 a night for a double. Options include a nine-course dinner of French cuisine ($17 a person) and a hot-air-balloon safari at dawn followed by breakfast ($200 a person).

The next day we arrive at the Mara River, which is slow and brown, lined with palm trees and marsh grass and, in some places, high bluffs. Below, eyes and noses of hippopotamuses float in the still water. With a gurgle, one nose disappears, leaving a circle of bubbles. Beside a mud bank, the scaly back of a crocodile breaks the surface of the brown water, then silently submerges.

Later, at the edge of the cold, clean swimming pool ($3 for non-guests) of the

Mara Serena Lodge, we sip iced drinks and chat with other vacationers, mostly Europeans and Americans carrying cameras and binoculars and wearing khaki-colored safari clothes. We see no African guests here or anywhere else in Kenya's game parks. Indeed, the prices of lodge accommodations, organized safari tours, or even car rentals are well beyond the reach of most Kenyans.

Partly to see more of the Kenyan people and partly because we aren't on a typical visitor's budget, we get directions to a workers' canteen behind the Serena Lodge for dinner. It is a single room lit by kerosene lamps and furnished with tables and benches, about half-full of African men and women, who become silent and stare as we enter. Then a young man steps forward with courtesy and aplomb and escorts us to a table, handing us menus hand-printed in Swahili and explaining the dishes in English. Over plates of cornmeal porridge, brown beans, spinach, and spicy tomato sauce ($1 a person), we practice Swahili, to the open smiles of people at neighboring tables. Suddenly everyone wants to help us. "You must learn the Masai greeting also," one man prompted proudly. We learn that most of them stay on the reserve for a month or more at a time without visiting their families, but that the relatively high wages make park jobs highly sought after.

On our map we mark the shortest distance to our next destination, Lake Naivasha, but in Kenya, shortest is not necessarily quickest. In five hours of bumping along rutted, washed-out roads, we have two flat tires and get stuck hub-deep in dust and laugh bitterly at each other's gray skin, lips, hair, and clothes. For once we want a hotel with a hot shower, but the splendid Safariland Lodge on the lakefront charges the customarily high lodge rate. "Isn't there something else?" The lodge receptionist sends us to the town of Naivasha to Bell's Inn, a middle-class hotel with colonial architecture and, except for us, African patrons. Neat, clean rooms look out on a newly mowed courtyard. But a water pipe is broken, the manager tells us apologetically, and each room has only enough water to fill the sink.

Out on the lake the next day, hundreds of pearly flamingos open their wings with a flash of scarlet; handsome fish eagles circle and dive; dozens of exotic bird

following pages: *With its stark contrast, it is amazing to note that each zebra's markings are unique and one of a kind.*

Mama and baby elephants enjoy a mud bath.

200

IF YOU GO

Many airlines offer connections to Nairobi. The best times to visit are during the dry seasons, July through October and January through April. Visas, required for U.S. citizens, are available from the Kenyan Embassy in Washington. Contact the Kenya Tourist Office, 424 Madison Ave., 6th floor, New York, NY 10017, (212) 486-1300.

species are seen nesting along the reeds. And, feeling the clean lake breeze in our faces, we think Lake Naivasha is worth the trip.

We arrive at Amboseli National Park covered, as usual, with a mud made of dust and sweat. Badly eroded orange soil blows between stones the size of footballs that cobble the land as far as we can see. Across the Tanzanian border, suspended blue against the blue sky, is 19,340-foot Mt. Kilimanjaro, its white cap shining like a snowball.

By now we have established a basic course of action: pitch our tents, and head for the lodge. Sipping cold drinks on the terrace of Amboseli Serena, we watch a herd of shy impala approach hesitantly, drink from the stream less than 50 feet away, and quickly trot back across the plain. As sunset streaks the sky with purple and rose, a single elephant calmly advances.

Because we have only a few more days of our safari tour, we fall to reminiscing with other guests, trying to hold on to images of the magnificent animals we've seen wandering at will through their native land.

Mother cheetah teaches her cub in the badly eroded orange soil.

Closer to Home

America's Diversity, at Eye Level

Midwestern Playground:
Lake Michigan's Eastern Shore

Saratoga Springs:
Victorian Charm and
a Fabled Past

Sonora Museum
Makes it Easy to Find
Desert Wildlife

Amish Country

Daniel B. Wood

AMERICA'S DIVERSITY, AT EYE LEVEL

RIDING THE NATION'S HIGHWAYS ISN'T WHAT IT USED TO BE. SURE, "Burma Shave" signs are gone, though "Stuckey's" is still there. You already know about the family farm.

In 1986, a journey across America is still a journey of toll booths and cloverleafs, glittering cityscapes, and franchised food.

It is still towering woodlands, amber prairies, and majestic mountains, punctuated with moccasin shops and signs hawking saltwater taffy. It is still a journey of squinting between billboards for three-letter signs (GAS, OIL, EAT) and destination-markers (Myrtle Beach, next left).

But experienced at eye level rather than from 30,000 feet for the first time in 20 years, a trip across America is mostly a trip of spontaneous discovery—the smell of a Louisiana bayou, the sizzle of a Santa Fe sidewalk. It is also, alas, laced with an unavoidable cliché: America, the land of urban sprawl. (Yes, Joni Mitchell, "They paved paradise, put up a parking lot.")

If there is one observation that dominates all others, it is the arrival—everywhere—of the mall.

If the last time you crossed America was in your parents' '57 Chevy, you might well find that the little souvenir stand on your favorite ribbon of highway has been replaced by a mall.

The roads ahead hold the majesty of the continental divide.

left: *Amber prairies at sunset.*

The winding road is dwarfed by the magnificent canyons of Montrose County, Colorado.

You can read William Kowinski's *The Malling of America* to get the statistics. There are more shopping centers in the United States than movie theaters, more enclosed malls than cities, four-year colleges, or television stations—and nearly as many malls as county courthouses. But even the malls have their regional trappings: conservative in Boston, large in Texas, funky in California.

Though you may inhale America in one breath, you exhale awed descriptions of size, shape, and diversity. We saw the lights of the Eastern Seaboard dim into backroad forests across the rural South. Stark plains of ice-covered sagebrush and sienna-hued buttes across the Southwest give way to sandy desert in Death Valley then feather-duster palm trees and orange-groves in southern California.

It's no brilliant observation that accents, attitudes, and language usage change, too. It's fun to see it happen in one fell swoop. "How do you do?" (Boston), "Howdy y'all" (Alabama), "Hey, Dude" (Los Angeles). A 3,000-mile drive in 10 days, by virtue of speed and superficiality, does tend to reinforce regional stereotypes—the boasting Texan, the flaky Californian. But by placing each in a broader context of others, you can see most stereotypes are exaggeratedly drawn composites.

That observation excludes Southern policemen. As I stepped off the curb to jaywalk in Dallas, a motorcycle cop zoomed into my path and impaled me with steely glare: "Go down to the crosswalk!" he said from behind mirrored aviator glasses. He didn't say, "You in a heap o' trouble, boy," but he might as well have.

If accents and attitudes and landscape are regional, so are cars. Having left mittened-and-scarved Bostonians wrestling Christmas trees atop family station wagons, we saw the evergreens stuffed into Jeep Wagoneers, four-wheel drive Blazers, and Broncos across the West. In Beverly Hills, we saw the trees plopped into convertible Mercedeses and Rolls-Royces by people in Hawaiian shirts and sunglasses beneath sunny, dry skies.

Next to malls on the list of the transcontinentally obvious is the proliferation of franchises: Wendy's, Burger King, Long John Silver's, Aamco, etc. For those Americans once bothered by their domination of the main strips leading in and out of every large city—each strip a stultifying clone of the one before—they can now contemplate the new, homogenized look as it engulfs smaller towns: Greenville, SC, Tuscaloosa, AL, Meridian, MS.

The trend may be neither new nor significantly different from previous years. What seems more compelling is what has been elbowed aside in the process.

Enamored by one mom-and-pop restaurant/inn in our first night in Perrysville, DL, the Douglass Motor Inn, where Helen and Jones Douglass have given personal attention to travelers for over 50 years, we endeavored to search out family-run establishments the rest of the way. We never saw another one from Baltimore to Los Angeles.

The most obvious regional differences in food are differences in the appearance of food chains. Krystal's Hamburgers, Popeye's Fried Chicken, and a greater variety of taco stands begin to appear in the Southern states. Pull over in your car after penetrating the city limits of many a town, and ask some locals where to get a real good taste of regional food, and you get a lot of blank stares.

That excludes Louisiana, where Cajun and Creole restaurants abound— and some stretches of Texas, New Mexico, and Arizona, where Mexican and New Mexican cuisines and good ol' American steak houses thrive.

Again, with deference to William Least Heat Moon (whose bestseller, *Blue*

Highways, chronicled America from the back roads) and Charles Kuralt (whose CBS broadcasts celebrate the diversity of off-the-beaten-path America), this is how it looks from the main roads.

The biggest general change-of-scene from east to west is, beginning somewhere around Texas, space.

Says Moon, who spent a year traveling back roads: "The vast openness changes the roads, towns, houses, farms, crops, machinery, politics, economics and, naturally, ways of thinking."

Whether or not they reduce man's blindness to the immensity of the universe around him, as Moon avers, the wide open spaces do, out of an increasing sense of exile and unconnectedness, push him toward a greater reliance on himself, and toward a greater awareness of others and what they do. Even speeding across the Southwest, the distances do eat you up.

One last comment: Read America's regional newspapers to be reminded that news affects real people there. Mrs. Greene at 415 Main Street, for instance, whose shoestore will be closing after 50 years because of competition by a national franchise. School overcrowding, farmers in crisis, and interest rates all take effect there before the metropolitan newswriters piece events together and call it a trend. And you find the reason that so much of the "significant" news is generated in so-called large metropolitan news capitals: That's where the correspondents are stationed.

After a full trip of 350-mile days, gaining an hour, by the way, on three separate occasions as you move west, you can really appreciate the richness and diversity of Los Angeles—in landscape, architecture, and activity.

Crossing the bottom of Death Valley and the Mojave Desert en route to "Lotus Land", you see the ring of rust-colored smog hanging over the city like a pot lid, easily mistakable for a golden sunset by the uninitiated.

It's while looking out at the Pacific rather than the Atlantic that you realize that somewhere between "Hahvid Yahd" and Hollywood, the rules changed. Brownstones gave over to stilt houses, wingtips and Weejuns evolved into roller skates or thongs, and "what's proper" changed from table manners to jacuzzi etiquette. Where did it happen? Alabama, Texas, New Mexico?

Thus we found out: Those who cross America at high speeds are liable to miss it. Those who go in search of answers may come back with more questions:

Forget the Alamo, who are the Cajuns?

Who were the five civilized tribes and where are they now?

Was California once part of Mexico?

Why is Texas so big?

The answer to America is to keep going back, go slow, and be sure to take a guidebook.

following page: *In our rich tapestry of language use, a "Howdy y'all," from Alabama or "Hey, Dude,' from Los Angeles would be heard on Boston's Beacon Hill as "How do you do."*

L. Dana Gatlin

MIDWESTERN PLAYGROUND: LAKE MICHIGAN'S EASTERN SHORE

ANYONE LOOKING FOR A SUMMERTIME SLICE OF AMERICANA COULD do worse than explore the green eastern shore of Lake Michigan. Here is where people from the nation's heartland come to play.

To play, and to escape the torrid heat of Detroit and Chicago and the Midwestern plain a few hundred miles to the south. Even before you reach Muskegon and the southern reaches of the Manistee National Forest, the land begins to grow greener.

It isn't long before rolling hills, tall trees, and lakes of all sizes surround you. They form a natural backdrop for fishing for coho salmon, listening to a summer concert at Interlochen's National Music Camp, or exploring the Sleeping Bear Dunes National Lakeshore. And in early summer, you can devour cherries in what is possibly every form they come in.

As is often the case, however, what really sets this region apart is the people—both those who come to play and those who make everything ready. At the risk of oversimplifying, there is a certain well-fed squareness in the physique of many Midwesterners that is often accompanied by directness in manner and a kind of "what-you-see-is-what-you-get" look in the eyes. The result can be a waitress, an innkeeper, or a motel clerk who gives you the feeling that somehow

left: *Lake Michigan at sunset.*

you've gotten to know him or her as a fellow human being.

The value of this warmhearted Michigan approach to people was made obvious at the beginning of our vacation. At the tip of the peninsula dividing Grand Traverse Bay from the main body of Lake Michigan is Northport, and it was here we arrived on one of the biggest weekends of the year, smack in the middle of the cherry harvest. Without any reservations, we were about to become impromptu campers, but Kay Charter at Hutchinson's Garden Bed and Breakfast took pity on us and sent us to see Violet Hall.

Hall is a lovely little octogenarian who grew up on the corner next to what is now the Empire National Bank. That's only half a block from the neat white house where she lived for decades, across the street from a grassy park at the edge of the town beach marina.

Since Hall no longer actively solicits guesthouse business, we were overjoyed to find we passed inspection. We were assigned a nice, fully equipped cottage with a view of the bay and two great shade trees in the park across the street. These were the same trees, Hall told us, which 70-some years ago bore twin tree houses—one for her, one for her brother—to which her mother regularly delivered afternoon cookies.

On our first night on the Grand Traverse Bay we attended a "fish boil" under those trees. A festive tent had been set up by the fire department and, as the sun set, we took part in a wonderful native feast. Lake Michigan "whitefish" is a breed purportedly unique to these waters, and when it is skillfully simmered with new potatoes, onions, and other local delights and shared at long tables with cherry farmers, locals, and tourists—well, it is a delicious taste of Michigan's lake country.

Violet's son is a fisherman; he brings his boat back from Florida in the summer. We came upon him cleaning big, silver salmon; chinook, he said. He had caught them on a trolling rig at the startling depth of 90 feet. These lake salmon feed only where the water temperature is 52 degrees. Normally, that would be at 30 feet, but in a truly hot summer, you need to troll 60 feet deeper.

Those who wish to try their skill with Lake Michigan's kings—coho, steelhead, and lake trout, depending on the season—will find charter services at various ports. A full day's outing for two people should cost $85 to $100 per person, a half day (five hours) perhaps $55.

If you really want a slice of Lake Michigan Americana, however, take in the various local parades and excuses to celebrate summer in this "cherry capital of the world."

Last year, in honor of the National Governors' Conference at Traverse City, about 200,000 people lined up all day and evening for a piece of "the world's biggest cherry pie"—at least that was the *Guinness Book of World Records* mark

IF YOU GO
For more details about travel anywhere in Michigan, call (800) 5432-YES.

everyone was shooting for. The pie came out of a vat 18 feet across—it's still on display—which required a ladder to see into.

On our way back, we visited the Sleeping Bear Dunes National Lake Shore, near Glen Arbor. This 71,000-acre preserve provides a marvelous overlook of Lake Michigan. Sand dunes up to 200 feet high, though shrinking every year, are a dramatic illustration that Lake Michigan is a product of the Ice Age, the remnant of a receding glacier.

Prevailing southwesterly winds and waves have formed the dunes at a point 54 miles across the great lake from Wisconsin. According to Chippewa Indian legend, long ago a mother bear and her two cubs were driven into Lake Michigan by a forest fire. After swimming many hours, the cubs tired, but the mother reached shore and climbed to the top of a high bluff to watch and wait for them. When they didn't appear, the great spirit Manitou created two islands to mark where they disappeared and a solitary dune to represent the faithful mother bear.

Now, it seems only a matter of time until the eroding winds and shifting sands cause "the bear" to disappear. It is a fitting vantage point for a farewell look at Lake Michigan.

Sand dunes up to 200 feet high, though shrinking every year, are a dramatic illustration that Lake Michigan is a product of the Ice Age, the remnant of a receding glacier.

Hilary DeVries

SARATOGA SPRINGS: VICTORIAN CHARM AND A FABLED PAST

ALTHOUGH DIAMOND JIM BRADY ROLLED INTO TOWN NEARLY A century ago in a silver-plated railroad car staffed with 27 Japanese houseboys (no gift for understatement, that Jim), mere mortals tend to put a slightly less tony foot to Saratoga turf today.

And with good reason. This legendary Adirondack spa that gained popularity with its stream of naturally carbonated spring water and a slew of antebellum, high-society visitors is currently appealing to more than the social-register set.

Thanks to vigorous historic preservation and the 20-year-old Saratoga Performing Arts Center (SPAC), the town is off and running with yet another chapter in its gilt-edged, 200-year-old history. In 1986, the National Museum of Dance, the only museum in the country devoted exclusively to that subject, opened its doors in the newly renovated 1924 Washington Bathhouse.

Every summer this normally sleepy Hudson River town snaps to life with the annual influx of seekers after Saratoga's unique blend of culture, horses, and history. This one-time "Queen of Resorts," which counted Lillian Russell and Commodore Vanderbilt among its patrons, now hosts annual visitors ranging from the highbrow set to the Honda crowd.

left: *Overnight guests at the Adelphi Hotel experience the high life —Victorian style.*

214

The Historical Society Museum, located in Congress Park, is one of the best places to experience Saratoga's history.

Certainly high society sweeps in for four manic weeks in August, drawn by its own tradition and avid interest in Saratoga's famous horse races. The city's Victorian appeal—many of the vintage buildings and homes date from early- to mid-19th century—is capped by the cupolaed clubhouse at the 122-year-old Saratoga Race Course. The oldest active thoroughbred racetrack in the United States, the course reigns as the dowager of American racing fields. And during August, Saratoga *is* horse country, with everything from harness racing to yearling sales and polo matches available to the public.

Much of Saratoga's allure, however, stems from its distinctly hybrid nature—part raffish river town, part college town (Skidmore College), part social register, and part small town, USA. During a visit in one of the most popular weeks, I found Saratoga a unique, hospitable, and surprisingly unpretentious resort with more than horses up its sleeve.

The downtown is laid out on an axis, surrounding Congress Park—site of the Museum of the Historical Society of Saratoga Springs in the former Canfield Casino—and this is where visitors should aim. Entering town on South Broadway requires a brief but dismal drive past the usual roadside clutter—gas stations, fast-food outlets, cut-rate motels, and the like. But don't let this deter you from the treasure-trove of Victorian architecture.

Saratoga's two grand hotels—the Grand Union and the United States—are long since gone, but the Adelphi Hotel still stands as a historical reminder. A stay here, or even just a stop for lunch or supper, is a trip back to the gay nineties. The lobby, alone, is furnished with enough bibelots, draped velvet curtains, and damask sofas to make Dickens's Miss Havesham feel right at home. A few visitors might find the Adelphi a bit *too* much in period.

The two best places to get the lowdown on the town's history are the Saratoga Circuit Tour, a once-a-day, two-hour minibus excursion leaving from an office one block north of the Adelphi Hotel and the Historical Society Museum in Congress Park. Despite Saratoga's compact size—only 20,000 year-round residents—the city boasts a rich and varied history, ranging from a pivotal Revolutionary War battle (the monument is located just a mile or two outside town) to the invention of the potato chip.

The Historical Society Museum will fill in the rest of the gaps of Saratoga's glory days as a renowned resort. There are black-and-white shots of the grand hotels, and of a few fancy-dress balls, as well as a couple of original Saratoga Springs's water bottles (bottling of the waters is no longer permitted). Another exhibit includes an original Saratoga trunk—that camel-backed valise preferred by wealthy summer visitors and disparaged by porters for its unstackability.

On your way out of the museum and Congress Park, stop for a horse-drawn carriage ride and taste the "zesty" water at the Hawthorn No. 1 spring (one of

right: Prof. Moriarty's is one of many charming restaurants in downtown Saratoga.

eight remaining springs in the city proper) on the corner of Spring and Putnam streets. We found it almost undrinkable, although the attendant assured us, "This is what Perrier wants."

One block north of Spring is Phila Street, the home of Mrs. London's Bake Shop—one of Saratoga's most recommended eateries. We started the day with a café-style breakfast here over white linen and Villeroy and Boch china, with a strolling banjo player whose renditions of "Camptown Races" made August in Saratoga seem more like Louisville, KY, at Derby time.

For a taste of everyday Saratoga we delayed our visit to the Spa State Park for an hour or so and strolled about town window-shopping and visiting local shops. Despite its flashy reputation, Saratoga is refreshingly devoid of plush boutiques and deluxe hotels. With the exception of the annual yearling sales, there isn't much here on which to drop one's cash. A fifties clothes shop-cum-hair salon, an old-fashioned barber-shop (complete with barber poles), and a dark, low-ceilinged antique bookstore are about it. One antique shop on Broadway—in a former bank building complete with safes—contained imported English pine furniture, about the only items in town that ran to four figures. Thirty other antique dealers are housed in the Museum of Antiques and Art of Saratoga Springs on Regent Street.

After a quick drive up Broadway for a *de rigueur* view of the mansions of the old racing families and a tour around Skidmore College's new, wooded 1,200-acre campus, we headed out to the Spa State Park. The 2,200-acre park, commissioned by Franklin D. Roosevelt, then governor of New York, was designed by financier Bernard Baruch as an extension of the original Saratoga Springs Reservation. The towering pines lining the drive make for an elegant entrance to the sprawling park that includes on its grounds the famous mineral spring baths, two pools, two golf courses, several clay tennis courts, and the Gideon Putnam Hotel—all of which are open to the public, and with the exception of the hotel in high season, amazingly reasonable in price.

We lunched on the terrace of this famous, white-columned hotel, overlooking a sea of Rolls Royces. Afterward we strolled the grounds and found all the facilities underused—except the baths, which book up weeks in advance for August.

The Saratoga Performing Arts Center (SPAC) shares the grounds here. The 5,000-seat, open-air auditorium (an additional 20,000 can be seated on the lawn) is home in July for the New York City Ballet and in August for the Philadelphia Orchestra.

Those in search of the horsey pursuits should head north on Circular Street (rubbernecking again at the period houses) and then west on Union Avenue. You will pass the National Museum of Racing, noted for its exclusive devotion to the history of thoroughbred racing, and the famous racetrack itself. During race weeks, Union Avenue takes on a state-fair ambiance, with flag-waving parking attendants and traffic police. A seat in the cupolaed grandstand, decorated with window boxes of red and white geraniums, is worth fighting the crowds for, if for no other reason than to get a good look at its architecture. Breakfasting at the track in panama hat and binoculars, while watching the silky thoroughbreds work out, is a longstanding ritual among horse lovers.

A last stop on Union Avenue is Yaddo, the 39-year-old artists' colony that counts Edgar Allan Poe, John Cheever, and Leonard Bernstein among its alumni. The colony, once the estate of New York banker Spencer Trask, is now open year-round to a select number of artists. While the turreted main house is closed to the public, visitors may wander the spacious grounds.

For a scenic country drive, head out of town on Route 29, one exit north of Union Avenue on the New York State Throughway. This twisting, two-lane road takes you past Saratoga National Park, in which looms a 155-foot granite obelisk marking the site of Gen. John Burgoyne's 1777 surrender. Back on the road, head toward the country towns of Schuylerville and Greenwich, NY. Open the car windows, and let the winding New York farmland work its magic.

IF YOU GO

August in Saratoga can be hot, crowded, and overpriced, but the Chamber of Commerce can help with bookings: (518) 584-3255. Saratoga is four hours by car from New York City, three hours from Boston. Amtrak runs one train a day from New York City. Several airlines fly into Albany, 30 miles south of the city.

This one-time "Queen of the Resorts" still maintains a high Victorian charm and a fabled past.

Ellen Steese

SONORA MUSEUM MAKES IT EASY TO FIND DESERT WILDLIFE

IF YOU'VE NEVER BEEN TO THE SONORA DESERT, YOU CAN'T IMAGINE what a strange place it is. The mountains are covered with scrubby vegetation. They look mysterious, almost like headless camels. And the local plants are straight out of moviedom's special-effects department.

The wildlife is more familiar. Tarantulas, snakes, lizards, and coyotes do well here, of course, and in the higher elevations, bears, mountain lions, and mountain goats. In the more southern reaches of the desert, in Baja, California, you get some pretty fancy birds—thick-billed parrots, for instance.

As for plants, it takes a genuine oddball to survive here. Like the saguaro cactus—the plant that lets you know you're in the Sonora. Or the cholla cactus, whose flabby, grayish fruit can latch on to the unwary passerby with nasty prickers.

Over 300 different kinds of animals and 200 kinds of plants inhabit 15 landscaped acres, set in the heart of Tucson Mountain Park. Most zoos and botanical museums have to range far and wide to get specimens, but the Arizona-Sonora Desert Museum is strictly regional and proud of it. The curators don't even *water* their plants.

The great thing about the museum is that the local surroundings have been

The aerial view of the heart of Tucson Mountain Park where 300 species of animals and 200 of plants are hosted.

left: *The Praire Dog is a true greeter to the desert habitat.*

The wildlife is the familiar snakes, lizards, coyotes, and tarantulas.

compressed and intensified for you. A few of the plants you'll easily see elsewhere in Arizona, but as for the wildlife—you'd have to be a naturalist to find it.

And now the museum is doing its best to make you forget that it is a zoo at all. A new $2.5 million habitat has just opened, designed so that you can see white-tailed deer, mountain lions, brown bears, and other mountain animals, all in enclosures of convincing-looking fake rock, with the natural mountain backdrop behind them.

This is part of a grand reorganization plan to take place as funds are available over the next few decades. The old format showed caged animals sorted by classification: snakes with snakes, cats with cats, and so on. The modern approach is putting predators and prey and the plants that go with them, close together in a natural setting.

Elevation is the critical factor here, not because of the difference in heat but the difference in water, according to Christopher Helms, development and public affairs officer. The new habitat represents the desert's highest elevation, and it features, among other plants, 200-year-old Arizona white oak trees and some magnificent "evergreen oaks," as they are called here, all transplanted from a rancher's land.

Building a new museum like this is strictly a custom job. "These exhibits are different from those that exist anywhere else," said Helms. For one thing, there is no guarantee that the animals' needs and the designer's ideas will coincide. The talk of the museum the week I was there was the pranks of two five-month-old bears. First, one bear caused a furor by almost staging a getaway. Then both bears gave a keeper the shock of her life when she happened upon them in the neighboring den for the gray foxes who hadn't moved in yet; their area was designed to be mercifully bear-proof. (Both escape hatches have since been redesigned.)

Peter Siminski, curator of birds and mammals, took me for a behind-the-scenes tour. There's something enchanting about seeing a zoo with an insider; the animals all come trooping over to you. An exception was one of the jaguarundis, a recent mother; she bared her fangs at me—a savage red and white snarl in a small chocolate-colored face.

We visited the animals' kitchen, which included a walk-in freezer full of, among other things, great bags of Purina Dog Chow. It was the animals' monthly "goodie day," so plates of special raw meats were everywhere.

He led me over to the cage of the vampire bats—small furry balls hanging upside down. They have nasty expressions and are fed bowls of blood at mealtime, according to Siminski.

We also passed a cage containing three elf owls, sitting on their perch. Spying us, they abruptly drew themselves up to their full four inches, swiveled

right: Bears frolicking for the gallery.

222

their heads toward us, opened their eyes wide, and froze. They looked like something ceramic you'd buy in a gift shop.

"When will they straighten out?" I asked, as the owls locked into position.

"Oh, they will, *eventually*," said Siminski casually as we walked off, leaving them to it.

At the time of my visit the animals in the new habitat were just getting used to their quarters. "We have to get animals used to their enclosures so that they know where they live," said Siminski. This procedure is complicated when there is more than one species in an enclosure, because each species has to first get used to its cage, then to the outer, public area; then both species must be put together so they can get used to each other.

We went behind the scenes to the cage area to see the mountain lion, who was at that point in the "cage stage" of the adjustment process. The bears came back into their cage area to have a look at us.

Bears like to play to the gallery. One stuck his nose through the bar in an aren't-I-adorable sort of way, then rolled back on a small fat rump, giving a great impersonation of a bear who would never in his wildest dreams think of biting anybody. "Bears can sucker you; watch out," Siminski said warning me as we went by.

Giant saguaro is often seen in the American Southwest.

IF YOU GO
For more information about the Sonora Desert Museum call
(602) 883-1380.

The mountain lion had just lost his mate and was sitting alone in his new cage. His opinion of the situation was expressed in the low set of his ears, a resigned look in his steady golden eyes, and in a certain lack of animation about the tail. He seemed glad to be visited though and began making an irregular hoarse growling noise that Siminski said was the sound of a mountain lion purring. "He likes you," he said.

A later phone call revealed that the lion is now out in his enclosure, has cheered up, and a new mate has been acquired for him. He has taken to living in his viewing window and interacting with visitors.

It is a wrench to tear yourself away from a purring mountain lion. But we went on to the museum's wonderful walk-through aviary. On our way, we wandered past a coyote, looking like a friendly husky dog grinning and squinting in the hot sun; fat prairie dogs, like overgrown hamsters, surrounded by a crowd of admirers; and a cardinal on top of an ocotillo. We also passed several docents, one with a beautiful owl on a leash, another holding a large turtle.

It was hot, and many of the birds you can usually see in the aviary were hiding, though we did see a magpie jay, with its sweeping tail of black- and- white diamonds. The birds seemed very happy here: "Lots of birds try to get *in*," said Siminski. The aviary is an example of the interaction between the museum and its environment. ``If you notice all the birds looking up, look up and you'll see a hawk.''

I said goodbye to Siminski and wandered around the museum for a while by myself. There are many strange and beautiful sights here. There is a room full of minerals like great lumpy jewels: azurite, flat plates of the brightest blue; malachite, fuzzy jade green blobs; tangerine colored wulfenite; and calcite, like frozen milk. Then I went outside again.

Talking to people here, you get a different view of the less likable animals and insects. I saw one man tenderly holding a gigantic tarantula in two thick, cupped hands. From him I learned that tarantulas—at least the North American varieties—are very remarkable and much maligned. They can live to be 25-30 years old, are docile, don't mind being picked up, and are not particularly dangerous even if tormented into biting, and are quite fragile. "If I dropped her, she'd probably die," he said, looking down at the motionless, doorknob sized beast, with its 5-inch long brown furry legs: the stuff of nightmares, squatting trustingly in his hands.

The Sonora Desert Museum was founded 33 years ago by a self-taught naturalist named Bill Carr, who thought of what was then the standard museum of natural history as a "dead animal museum," according to Helms.

"Most zoos are postage stamp collections," he says. But this one permits "a willing suspension of disbelief."

Suzanne Schiffman

AMISH COUNTRY

I KNEW IT WAS TIME TO SHED CITY WAYS AS I CAREFULLY THREADED my way through Don and Ginny Ranck's cow barn in my summer sandals to watch my three-year-old bottle-feed a calf.

We had arrived by car with our two small children to stay several nights at Verdant View, a working farm one mile east of Strasburg, in the heart of Pennsylvania Dutch country.

Our plan was to explore the area as much as possible by bike. We pulled up to the farmhouse about 5 o'clock, just in time to watch Ginny start the evening milking of the couple's 50-odd Holsteins.

Before we had even unloaded the car, much less seen our accommodations in the 1896 house, Heather, one of the Rancks' four children, invited our kids to help her feed the calves. We watched her fill several quart-size baby bottles with the fresh, warm milk and snap on huge nipples, then followed her through the barn to the calves, several of which were only a day or two old. They raised little heads at the first whiff of the milk and guzzled each bottle in about five seconds, to the delighted laughter of our children.

As we walked back through the barn and farmyard, we met the rest of the Ranck family's entourage—two goats, two dogs, nine cats, and five kittens. In the excitement of being able to touch and pet so many animals, our children forgot

Some of the huge working farms take in guests for the summer months.

left: *The Mennonites and their more conservative brethren, the Amish, are best known for their 18th-century life-styles.*

Lancaster County, PA; location
of Verdant View farm.

to start complaining about being tired and hungry after the car trip and settled down to play with the kittens in the yard.

When the Ranck children came out with balls and wagons, we knew this visit would be a success—the children were happy, and so were we.

Verdant View is just one of many working farms that take in guests in the area east of Lancaster during the summer. We found it through a guidebook, *Farm, Ranch, and Country Vacations*, by Pat Dickerman.

Our rooms on the second floor of the farmhouse were pleasant enough and airy, the furniture well-worn, and the decorations simple. The bathroom was huge, with an old claw-footed tub, and all the beds were covered with beautiful quilts handmade by local Amish women.

Breakfast was included in our room rate, and promptly at 8:30 the youngest Ranck child rang the breakfast bell. Guests join the family at one long table for scrambled eggs with fresh beef slices, apple crisp with "this morning's" milk, and toast with home-churned butter and homemade jam. The stories and conversations around the table each morning with the Rancks and other guests turned out to be one of the highlights of our trip.

Sometimes as many as 30 sit around the breakfast table, but in early April the number was more manageable—19. Most of the guests were families enticed by the idea of having their children take part in farm chores and learn about farm animals, in addition to being able to observe the Amish people.

The Rancks are Mennonites. These people, along with the more conservative Amish, are best known for their 18th-century lifestyle. Both sects fled religious persecution in Europe beginning in the 1720s, coming mainly from Holland and the Rhineland area of Germany and France. They found the rolling countryside of central and eastern Pennsylvania similar to their homeland, and settled here in large numbers. Today, there are about 40,000 Amish in North America, 14,000 of whom live in Lancaster County, according to the Pennsylvania Dutch Visitors Bureau.

Seven of the nine farms bordering the Rancks' are Amish-owned, and the owners pool their resources to buy up any farm or land that comes on the market. In 1975, Don Ranck took over the family farm started by his great-grandfather.

After most of the morning had slipped away, we reminded ourselves that our plan was to bike lazily through the back roads of Amish country, not sit at the farmhouse breakfast table.

We gathered up the children and began our bike ride at the Phillips Cheese Company parking lot in the town of Intercourse, seven miles northeast of Strasburg on state Route 340. Here, incidentally, you can watch workers make Swiss, Cheddar, Gruyére, and other cheeses in 300-gallon copper kettles.

Most of Lancaster County's secondary roads are suited to biking. The heart

preceding pages: *Amish
farmers still work the fields with
teams of horses.*

of Amish country is a diamond-shaped section east and northeast of the city of Lancaster. A good road map of the area is a big help in planning your bike tour. We had in mind a 30-mile circuit between Intercourse and Bowmansville, but any variation is possible, and we chose to limit our ride to a leisurely two hours using this tour.

The biking in this area is exceptionally agreeable. There are low rolling hills, and the traffic we encountered in April was not a problem. Most of what one sees are Amish buggies moving at a slightly slower pace than our bikes. Our friendly waves were readily acknowledged by the farm families. The men were plowing fields with their horse teams, the women tidying the already immaculate yards by raking, planting, and mowing. The children were out, too, playing close to their busy, but attentive, parents.

From the cheese company, we followed Hollander Road north to New Holland, then doubled back along Shirk Road and circled west via Fusser School Road. There is indeed a school on this road, a one-room Amish schoolhouse and playyard. The schoolhouse door was open, and we were treated to a sight from early America: children of all ages seated at old wooden school desks, reciting lessons and writing on tablets. Out in the schoolyard, some of the younger children were playing a version of softball, their happy shrieks sounding like any modern playground. But, with the boys in black breeches and the traditional jet-black brimmed hats and the girls in ankle-length dresses with the white "Kapps," we felt we were somewhere else in history.

From there we pushed on toward the village of Mascot, noting the working mill and hex signs, and on to Intercourse, which offers a mini-mall of highly commercialized tourist gift shops and eating spots. Intercourse also has several shops featuring hand-sewn quilts. Many of the Amish farmhouses display quilts for sale, too.

From here we turned north and back to the cheese factory.

Restaurants

Dining out in Lancaster County is a bargain. Many of the restaurants are large "family" ones specializing in eye-opening smorgasbords. Not only are these copious buffets usually of an all-you-can-eat variety, but children under 2 and sometimes 3 are free. The food is simple, but good, and most of the fresh produce and dairy products come from the neighboring farms.

The smorgasbords in Amish country are based loosely on the tradition of "seven sweet, seven sour" elements in a meal. This explains the pots full of apple butter, relish, beets, pickles, and the ever-present shoofly pie made of molasses and sweet dough crumbs. At a restaurant called Hershey Farm, we ate ravioli, sausage with beans, pork with sauerkraut, fried chicken, turkey croquettes, several vegetables, potatoes, and salad, even sampling some of the pies, and our

following page: With its low rolling farmland and slow-moving buggies, Lancaster County is a picturesque place for biking.

Our bike route allowed us to savor wonderful views of unique American folk art.

230

bill for four came to $14.50.

Several of these "family style" eating establishments are scattered throughout Lancaster County.

Other attractions

Lancaster County is full of things to do.

The Strasburg Railroad operates a train of 19th-century coaches pulled along by a steam locomotive between Strasburg and Paradise, or you can visit the Railroad Museum of Pennsylvania and the Toy Museum close by.

Mill Bridge Village is a restored colonial village with a working water-powered 1738 gristmill where flourmaking is demonstrated.

Those not content with looking at Amish farms from the outside can visit the Amish Farm and House or the Amish Homestead on U.S. Route 30 east of Lancaster city.

A visit to Lancaster's farmers' market (Central Market on Pennsylvania Square) is a treat. It's open Tuesdays and Fridays. You see the horses and buggies tied to the iron rings lining the side of the market while the Amish sell their homemade sausages, cheeses, and other things inside.

Our greatest pleasure throughout our stay, however, was returning to our base, the farm. There were always new nooks and crannies for our young children to explore. The Rancks, busy tending fields of hay and corn, cleaning barns, and milking cows, always found time to give their guests a warm welcome.

Holiday Happenings

For a Hispanic-Flavored
Holiday, Sample
San Antonio

A Newport Christmas

Dutch Christmas

On the Concorde,
a Supersonic Ride to the
Land of Reindeer

An Old Salem Christmas

Howard LaFranchi

FOR A HISPANIC-FLAVORED HOLIDAY, SAMPLE SAN ANTONIO

EVERY CHRISTMAS SEASON IN SAN ANTONIO, 1,600 *LUMINARIOS* ARE lighted along the Alamo City's famous River Walk. These votive candles, placed in sack-lunch-size paper bags and held in place by a few inches of sand, are a Southwestern tradition, symbolizing the celestial lights that greeted the Christ child. The flickering brown *luminarios* are one of many joys that San Antonio offers the yuletide visitor.

From just after Thanksgiving on into the new year, visitors here get a taste of a Christmas that is fashioned more after influences from the south—primarily Mexico—than from the north. The city's rich religious tradition is carried on through a number of pageants and festivals that may seem almost quaint in an era when the holiday season has taken on an ever-growing commercial edge.

But many travelers—whether on a short business trip, visiting family, or in town to see the many sites the nation's 10th-largest city has to offer—have noticed just how refreshing San Antonio in December can be. The malls and the frantic shoppers are here, of course, but somehow they seem easier to escape in a city where the season's religious traditions far outshine the commercial.

What makes the yuletide season in San Antonio worth a weekend trip or more is the city's strong Hispanic influences. These make for a Christmas that looks, feels, smells, and tastes different from the one most Americans know. San

Christmas at the Alamo in the heart of San Antonio.

left: *Thousands of lights twinkle in the trees along the River Walk.*

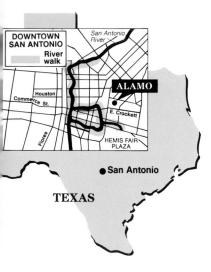

Downtown San Antonio,
highlighting River Walk, with
backdrop of the state of Texas.

Antonio is the largest city in the United States with a majority Hispanic population.

The season's red is more likely to be provided by dried hot peppers fashioned into a wreath than by English holly berries. Tamales, spiced hot chocolate, and Mexican cookies figure among the traditional foods. And in San Antonio, the jolly, rotund fellow in the red and white suit faces some friendly competition from a black-mustached, serape-draped Pancho Claus —the city's Hispanic equivalent of the legendary Santa Claus.

"Bringing out the Hispanic traditions is so much more appropriate for our climate than the snow and sleigh bells—that's stuff we've never seen," says Peggy Tobin, a member of the city's Conservation Society and an ardent supporter of the city's Christmas with a Spanish accent.

"Oh, I can remember when we used to put shaving cream on the windows to make it look like the North. But now we have a Christmas that fits our climate and our history."

One Christmas custom that's dear to San Antonians is *Las Posadas*, a pageant depicting the holy family's search for place to have their child. Continuing a Spanish tradition, the story has been told in the city's old missions and parishes for more than 250 years.

Beginning in the mid-sixties it was produced in the downtown area— initially as a booster of civic unity—and it has attracted local residents and their guests on a mid-December evening along the River Walk ever since.

"It was right about the time we were battling a major expressway they were planning to put through one of our nicest parks," says Lillian Padgett, a San Antonian who originated the idea of presenting Las Posadas downtown.

The city was torn over the freeway proposal, so Padgett—one of the road project's most unyielding critics—decided the pageant might be a way of bringing the city back together.

"The first year we only had about 30 people, but it has grown to something the whole community takes part in," she says, adding, ``We got the expressway route modified, too.''

Also a favorite is *Los Pastores*, Jan. 9-10, another traditional Spanish play that is presented at the city's San José Mission, one of five from the early 1700s that make up the San Antonio Missions National Historical Park. (The Alamo, in the heart of downtown, is also one of the missions.)

San José, known as "the queen of the missions of New Spain," is the perfect setting for the play that tells how the devil attempts—unsuccessfully of course!— to prevent the wise men, shepherds, and other pilgrims from reaching the Christ child.

San Antonio's Christmas season is actually kicked off the weekend of

Thanksgiving, when the city's mayor, Henry Cisneros, flips the switch on thousands of lights that twinkle in the trees along the River Walk, on which hotels and riverside restaurants and shops have been built. Following the lighting ceremony is a parade of brightly decorated river barges.

From then until Christmas, festivals and special holiday events are commonplace, especially in the city's churches. One rather special event that takes place just once, but which some visitors may not want to miss, is the blessing of the pets at El Mercado, a Mexican-style market.

Each year a Franciscan priest is asked, in the tradition of the nature-loving St. Francis, to bless the pets that are brought to the market. And each year El Mercado is turned into a temporary menagerie of birds, turtles, hamsters, snakes—and, of course, dogs and cats.

It is also at El Mercado that children may catch a glimpse of Pancho Claus, who brings greetings from the children of Mexico. A week-long Fiesta Navideña is scheduled to conclude Sunday in El Mercado.

To fill out the holiday festivities, visitors may choose from a number of possibilities, most of which are found in or near the downtown area.

A good start is the historic King William residential district, south of downtown, along the San Antonio River. Named after King William of Prussia, the area was developed in the late 1800s and includes a number of the city's finest old mansions. A huge flood in 1921 persuaded the moneyed classes to seek higher ground north of downtown, but after years of neglect the neighborhood is coming back. Some of the mansions are open, either for tours or as bed-and-breakfast accommodations, but it's also a nice area for a morning or afternoon stroll.

Another worthwhile stop is the San Antonio Museum of Art, home to one of the nation's finest collections of Mexican folk art. A 500-piece permanent exhibition offers a spirited and brightly colored glimpse of the many facets of an art form that maintains an important influence in San Antonio and the rest of the Southwest.

Also of interest is the San Antonio Botanical Gardens, which features plants from the Southwest, Mexico, and Central America. Of special note here is the unusual plant conservatory. The structure's partly underground greenhouses allow for taking advantage of the welcome winter sun, while protecting plants from the relentless heat of summer.

Of course the first-time visitor to San Antonio won't want to miss the Alamo, Texas' own cradle of liberty.

And for those visitors who can stretch their holiday visit to New Year's Eve, the city holds an annual party on the plaza in front of the Alamo. Food and entertainment, much of it with a Mexican flair, culminate in a fireworks display at midnight.

IF YOU GO
Additional information is available from the San Antonio Convention and Visitors Bureau, (800) 447-3372.

Continuing a 250-year tradition, Las Posadas, is dear to all San Antonians. It depicts the holy family's search for a place to have their child.

Ellen Steese

A NEWPORT CHRISTMAS

CHATEAU-SUR-MER IS A HANDSOME HOUSE, A VICTORIAN FORTRESS of a place, but it isn't the Newport mansion that usually dumbfounds the visitor. Except at Christmastime, that is, when it comes into its own.

This Italianate stone villa looks newer than the 18th-century-style mini-palaces around it, but actually it's a bit older. It was built in the 1850s, before the really aggressive architectural competition began among the society hostesses here. So the interior is warmer in feeling than those of the other mansions; it is grandmother's house—on a vastly more generous scale, of course.

The small rooms—by Newport standards—the jolly golden-oak Eastlake furniture and woodwork, the stained glass windows, the fanciful stenciled ceilings, the playful trellis pattern that runs up the open stairwell, make this a place for children.

It's a wonderful Christmas house. You can picture the four little Wetmores, children of the original owner, William Shephard Wetmore (governor of Rhode Island), running up and down the laurel-roped divided stairway. I feel sure they would have appreciated the fireplaces banked with holiday plants and the carved wooden mantels invisible under fir and holly, grapes and cones.

And the ceiling-high Christmas tree is a Victorian sure-fire hit: hung with

The grand entrance of the former Vanderbilt summer cottage, Marble House.

left: *Warmed by 500 plants, the Pointsetta tree in Marble House creates festivity for the gold leafed ballroom.*

The dining room at Chateau-sur-Mer in all her finest holiday decorations.

fans and angels, bouquets of dried flowers, Japanese lanterns, lavender ribbons, candles, and hearts stuffed with potpourri.

Chateau-sur-Mer was one of the few Newport mansions that was lived in year-round. Most of these flamboyant "summer cottages" were shut for the winter. When Mrs. Stuyvesant Fish and her group came for the season, what with servants, and friends and bags and baggage, it was like a small army on the move—not a journey to be undertaken more than once a year.

Thus, the Christmas decorations in Rosecliff are a fantasy of what Christmas might have been, had owner Theresa Fair Oelrichs and her guests spent the holiday at Rosecliff.

Oelrichs's father was one of the discoverers of the Comstock Lode, the richest silver mine ever found in Colorado, and she once gave a famous party in her cream-colored ballroom—to which all the ladies wore white dresses.

So Rosecliff, based on Versailles's Grand Trianon, traditionally decks the halls in snowy white. White poinsettias and paper narcissus line the famous heart-shaped staircase. More white blooms collect between the arched French windows of the ballroom, which look out on one side to green lawn and great stone urns and on the other to a stormy gray winter sea. White scallop shells, white lights, tinsel, and balls of sterling silver shine on the 18-foot tree in the peach damask salon.

I like to think that Newport's extravagant mansions take on—if such a thing is possible—almost a homey atmosphere at Christmas. Come to Rosecliff in the summer, and you keep visualizing F. Scott Fitzgerald lounging by the fountain (the *Great Gatsby* was filmed here, and echoes linger). But a house, any house, with a Christmas tree seems a place for family and friends.

The Elms, built by coal magnate, Edward Berwind, is a copy of the Chateau d'Asnieres, near Paris. Berwind could afford it; it was said that there wasn't a ship on any ocean that didn't use Berwind coal. Decorations in this house are intended to represent an Edwardian Christmas, in red and gold. I was told, though the color of the poinsettias this season is really pink. But they are everywhere—in front of statues, on the gold piano in the white salon, in the imperial-sized Chinese cachepots framing the grand marble stairs where you enter. The Berwinds died childless—and fortunately the house was saved from destruction by the Newport Preservation Society, which now owns and maintains all the mansions.

Nearby Marble House, home of the formidable Alva Vanderbilt, had a child living in it—the hapless Consuelo, who was once confined to her room upstairs, with its splendid but heavy English baronial furniture, so she couldn't escape before her wedding to the Duke of Marlborough.

Consuelo later defied her mother's social ambitions, divorced the Duke, and married a man she loved. But it's too bad it didn't happen here: Marble

House's gold ballroom is just the place for an 18-year-old to waltz blissfully until dawn. Gold leaf covers the walls, and gold faces peer down at you from above; there are two mighty gilded chandeliers, with trumpeting cherubs and forests of candles, and a mantel of fleur-de-peche marble surmounted by two bronze statues.

In December the mantel is shrouded in a welter of holiday red and greenery. But the pièce de résistance of the tour is the 18-foot Christmas "tree" of red poinsettias, 500 pots' worth, looking like a gigantic red bell.

There's no marble on the outside of Marble House—it's modeled after the Petit Trianon in Versailles; the two-store entrance hall of golden marble gives it its name. The dining room is marble, too—a light oxblood color. The centerpiece of the long table is a three-foot-high silver epergne of sheep and human figures surrounded by holly and red carnations.

If you drive along Newport's Bellevue Avenue, you can see these reminders of Versailles on either side of the road. There's the airy grace of Rosecliff—set back too far from the street for you to pick out the scallop shells and laurel adorning the gargoyles by the front door. And Chateau-sur-Mer, hiding its seasonal decoration within.

But you can pick out a few wreaths—classic green, with plain red bows—on the magnificent banklike fronts of Marble House and the Elms. And, in honor of the holiday season, these noble facades look friendly, almost welcoming.

IF YOU GO

All four houses are lit from dusk to 11. They are open only on weekends in the winter, from 10 a.m. to 4 p.m. For details contact the Preservation Society of Newport County, 118 Mill St., Newport, RI 02840, (401) 847-1000.

One of the few homes occupied year-round, Chateau-sur-Mer's grand tree in the ballroom uses lanterns, flags, and fans for ornaments.

Bunny McBride

DUTCH
CHRISTMAS

ARE YOUR CHRISTMAS "HOLI-DAYS" NO LONGER HOLY? ARE YOU weary of commercialism, hungry for a bit of peace on earth, goodwill toward one another? If so, you might consider spending Christmas in the Netherlands.

I did so last winter, joining my husband's family in the pastoral village of Glimmen, nestled in the northern part of the country. To my surprise, the twin hallmarks of an American Christmas—shopping and gifts—were absent. Instead there were simply family gatherings, accented with a wealth of special pastries, flowers, music, and church activities. Relatives and friends from all corners of the country stopped by to visit. Several days before Christmas, some of us attended a splendid Kerst-feest Oratorio (Christmas concert) in the 14th-century Martini Church that towers above the Netherlands' major northern city, Groningen.

Then, on a brisk and windy Christmas Eve, we sang time-honored Christmas hymns in a modest 13th-century church in the nearby town of Haren. And on Christmas morning, some of us rose early enough to bicycle to the village chapel for a Christmas service. For several days the skies rang with carols from chimes and carillons. The days were both cheery and hallowed, and it was easy to remember that centuries ago a life-changing event took place in Bethlehem.

But what of Santa Claus? I wondered. "You must mean Sinterklaas," my Dutch relatives told me. "To witness the festivities of Sinterklaas, you must come

"Have you been good?" Tradition says Sinterklaas listened through chimneys to check on children's behavior during the week before St. Nicholas Eve.

left: *Sinterklaas on horseback in his triumphant parade for adults and children alike.*

Christmas tree lighting in Gouda.

right: Skaters in the brisk December air.

to the Netherlands at least a month before Christmas, for here that celebration is an entirely separate occasion." And so it was that I discovered that Santa Claus (also known as Sinterklaas, St. Nicholas, Old St. Nick, Kriss Kringle, and Father Christmas, etc.) not only assumes different names from country to country, but also different characteristics, habits, and meanings. Yet all of these fellows share a common derivation.

Long ago there really was a man called St. Nicholas. He was born in the year 271 in the town of Pataras, in what is now Turkey. It is said that he was born to prosperous parents and that upon their death he decided to forfeit his wealth and dedicate his life to good works. Eventually he became bishop of the Christian Church in Myra, a city near his birthplace. His work was difficult, for he lived in a time when his part of the world was under Roman occupation and Christians were not popular. He rose to the challenge and became known as a fearless fighter for what he believed in. On one occasion, he interceded in the execution of three Roman soldiers who had been unfairly tried, and forced the provincial governor to set them free.

Nicholas died on Dec. 6, 342, and was buried in his own cathedral in Myra. His reputation for kindness and generosity gave rise to legends that ultimately made him one of the most revered of all Christian saints, and the patron saint of sailors and children.

In 1007, after Myra had fallen to the Muslims, a group of Norman sailors raided St. Nicholas's grave and transported his remains to Bari, in what is now southern Italy. From here, his fame spread throughout Europe.

St. Nicholas caught the eye of the seafaring Dutch because of his celebrity as the guardian of sailors. Gradually, his reputation as a benefactor to children became as vital as his role with seamen. Records from the 14th century show that choirboys received small gifts of money on St. Nicholas's feast day each Dec. 6. And convent school students received rewards or reprimands on that day by a teacher disguised as the venerable bishop.

By the 17th century, when most of the Dutch had turned from the Roman Catholic Church and embraced Calvinism, the religious overtones of the Catholic saint had been dropped and the name St. Nicholas had been corrupted to Sinterklaas. Still, in paintings, statues, parades, and imaginations, he remained dressed as the bishop he once was.

Today, Sinterklaas's feast day is celebrated with humor and fervor. Each year, come mid-November, the Dutch stage the steamboat arrival of their beloved bishop. When he lands in Amsterdam Harbor, it is understood that he has come all the way from Spain—considered to be his homeland ever since Bari, his resting place, fell under Spanish rule during the 16th and 17th centuries. For the past 24 years, an angelic-faced Amsterdam architect has portrayed Sinterklaas. The old

saint's proxy is welcomed with pomp and pageantry equal to that of a visiting head of state. I had the delight of witnessing the hoopla this year on Nov. 15.

By 10 a.m. that day, thousands of Dutch children and adults lined the borders of the canal that runs along the Prins Hendrikkade in front of the imposing Central (train) Station. Piped music of children singing Sinterklaas songs danced on the wind while the crowd sang, hummed, or tapped along. Hundreds of pigeons pirouetted overhead, and bells tolled in a nearby church tower.

"He's coming!" shouted a little boy perched atop his father's shoulders and waving a white flag that announced "Welcome Sinterklaas!" All eyes were riveted under the canal bridge.

When the nose of a yellow and green barge appeared, a hush swept across the crowd. In the ship's prow stood Sinterklaas, clothed in a red robe, topped by a white lace gown, a red brocade cape, and a tall red miter. He offered the crowd a benevolent and graceful wave. His playful Moorish helpmates, known as his Zwarte Pieten, surrounded him—all colorfully dressed in medieval puff trousers, tights, vests, and feathered velvet caps.

As Sinterklaas disembarked, the air vibrated and smoked with the booms of seven cannon shots. The stately saint then mounted his milk-white steed and began his parade through the city. Countless Pieten leaped, cartwheeled, and leapfrogged before and after Sinterklaas, while some 400,000 fans flanked the parade route.

In the weeks that follow this annual grand entrance, Sinterklaas and his Pieten have a major feat to accomplish: being all places at once. They (with the help of their "clones") visit schools throughout the country during the day, repeatedly posing that question of questions, "Have you been good?" Tradition says that at night they ride over the tile rooftops and listen through chimneys to double-check on the behavior of youngsters. Each night during the week before Dec. 5, St. Nicholas Eve, children sing songs by the fireplace, write notes to the good holy man, and place carrots or bits of hay in their shoes for his horse—hoping to find a "sugar animal" or some other small candy gift in their shoe the next morning.

On St. Nicholas Eve itself, the Zwarte Pieten deliver a sack full of presents for the whole family and their friends, to reward all who have been good. A Sinterklaas present is not at all like a Christmas present three weeks early. The gifts are far less extravagant than most Christmas presents in the United States, and Dutch tradition demands that each gift be accompanied by a poem written especially for the receiver. Whatever the length or quality of these poems, they are usually playfully mocking, urging everyone to laugh at themselves. The most common gift is a foot-long speculaas (lover)—a spice cookie in the form of a man or woman, given to one's sweetheart.

In 1613, the Dutch founded the American colony of New Netherlands and brought with them their Sinterklaas traditions. After the English took over that colony in 1664, renaming it New York, the image of Sinterklaas gradually merged with that of the roly-poly English Father Christmas, whose fete was the same month. Eventually Santa Claus (a direct derivation of Sinterklaas) and gift-giving became one with Christmas in the New World. Then, aided and abetted by other ethnic influences, the American Santa Claus myth developed to the point where he is now stationed at the North Pole, drives a sleigh pulled by reindeer, and spearheads the largest shopping campaign in the world.

Now that I've celebrated Christmas and Sinterklaas as two distinct events, I question the wisdom of the early Americans who merged them. Inevitably, the importance of Christmas as a time for quiet reflection gets lost in the hustle and bustle of American Santa Claus festivities. So much so that when we Americans walk through a store and hear "Silent Night" playing as background music, our first thought is not "peace on earth," but "Oh my goodness, I haven't started my Christmas shopping!" The Dutch are saved from this curious ambiguity. If you visit that country one December, you will see what I mean.

IF YOU GO

Contact the Netherlands National Tourist Office, 355 Lexington Ave., New York, NY 10017, or call (212) 370-7360 for more information.

A canal bridge cloaked in the early snows of winter.

Christopher Andreae

ON THE CONCORDE, A SUPERSONIC RIDE TO THE LAND OF REINDEER

ON CHRISTMAS DAY A COUPLE OF YEARS AGO SHE WAS ONE OF 96 passengers to fly by Concorde from London to Finnish Lapland. Now "I recommend it everywhere I go," she says.

This seasonal day trip, a two-hour flight each way, 12 hours in toto, is pure fantasy. The Concorde travels faster than sound and climbs so high that (as she recalls it) "through the windows you could see the complete curvature of the earth—just like a round ball, and you were on the edge of this round ball."

Once in Lapland, Mrs. Beacon-Lambert and the other passengers were driven through "Oh, beautiful wonderland scenery with all the log cabins, and all the log fires alight on the snow." (Nine times out of 10 you can be sure of a white Christmas in this part of the world.)

They drank hot reindeer milk and had their faces and necks rubbed with ice during a special crossing ceremony at the Arctic Circle. They went for rides down "a large river" on sleighs or snowmobiles. They had a meal with a choice of "50 dishes," including reindeer meat. And they were given presents made of Lapland silver: "cuff links for my son and all the men," and for Beacon-Lambert and the other women, silver necklaces. "It has a dove on it which I presume is for peace,"

The Concorde about to take off.

left: *A Lapp readies his team for the "Reindeer Safari."*

The Lapps, numbering no more than 30,000 are nomadic and each year follow their large reindeer herds from the mountains to the coastline.

she says. (Jan Knott of Goodward Travel, Canterbury, organizers of the flights, says it actually represents the Concorde.)

Best of all, Beacon-Lambert says, was the fact that they met "the real Santa Claus." At least she was convinced that his beard, which she " held onto," was genuine—though official sources deny this. With typical journalistic skepticism, I asked Boris Taimitarha, head of the London office of the Finnish Tourist Board, if he could tell me the true identity of the man who—year round—is the official Lapland Santa Claus. He phoned Rovaniemi, Finland, where the Concorde lands, to ask. The answer: "They say they wish to keep a certain mystery about him and so cannot reveal his name." But he confirmed that he has his own post office from which he replies to the children who write to him throughout the year.

The Christmas Concorde flights, in their fourth year, cost ú1,195 ($2,199) a seat—not as expensive as might be thought of when compared with the cost and journey time of ordinary flights on the same route—up to ú631 ($1,161) and 14 hours round trip.

The flights are always fully booked, and Goodward Travel has a long waiting list. To the enthusiastic Beacon-Lambert, "It was worth every penny we spent on it. … Mind you," she adds, and her voice does not suggest ostentatious wealth, "we're not rich people."

Mr. Knott expects the Laplanders will turn out, as at previous Christmases, to welcome the plane. "The first time about 20,000 Laplanders came to see us arrive—something like 90 percent of the population of Rovaniemi," he says. "And they still come."

Mr. Taimitarha confirms Concorde's great welcome in Lapland. Nobody seems to object to the aircraft's notorious noise, he says. "That might have been the question, maybe and I only say 'maybe'—in Helsinki, but up in Rovaniemi you are really in the middle of the wilderness."

Beacon-Lambert was warned by friends that the Concorde would be noisy and claustrophobic, but neither she nor her son, daughter, nor son-in-law, who were on the same flight, found either criticism valid.

Jackie Bassett, organizer of the Concorde Fan Club in Bath, agrees whole-heartedly. She has spent many years persuading detractors of Concorde that it is not noisy and dirty. She says she also feels strongly that it should not be only for the very rich. She has been in the field of offering charter flights on the aircraft longer than anyone else, and regrets that cutthroat competition is now creeping into the business.

This year she organized a Christmas special on the Concorde with a Christmas dinner on board, but "no Father Christmas" at ú369 ($678) a seat.

"I cater for Mr. and Mrs. Average," Bassett said.

This early Christmas flight did not land anywhere, but for added excitement the passengers were to have Christmas crackers (noisemakers) to pull (security officials permitting). They pulled them last year, all together, with one loud bang, just as the plane broke the sound barrier.

But it seems that Goodward Travel has the lion's share of Christmas Concorde flights. The pity is that they are too expensive for most people to take children. Knott estimates that only "10 to 15 percent" of the passengers are children, although "on one flight we had three generations of a family." On another, the grandparents treated their grandchildren, who didn't know they were going along until they were handed their tickets at the airport. They thought they had just come to see their grandparents off. I asked Beacon-Lambert, who sounds quite youthful on the telephone, how old her son was when she took him on the flight.

"How old?" she sounded puzzled. "Oh, he's 54," she answered, laughing. "And I'm 76."

IF YOU GO

For current information on flights and costs contact Goodward Travel in Kent, CT1 2QZ England, or call 0227 763 336 in England.

Two of the fleet-footed animals that whisk adventurous vacationers on the unique "Reindeer Safaris" at the Arctic Circle in Finnish Lappland, take five, while a Lapp guide keeps an eye on them.

Anne Crosman

AN OLD SALEM CHRISTMAS

THE HOLIDAY CELEBRATION HERE ATTRACTS MANY OF THE SAME visitors year after year, who come back to share in this community's slow and gentle breathing in of Christmas.

Old Salem is a restored, 18th-century Moravian village within the city of Winston-Salem. Small by Williamsburg, VA, standards—only 72 acres—it has a charm that draws smaller, more manageable crowds. The homes and craft shops are beautifully preserved. Old Salem marks Christmas the way the Moravians did 200 years ago. They stopped work briefly to make special candles and crèches, to listen to Moravian bands play carols, and to go to a church love feast (the agape meal of Biblical tradition) on Christmas Eve.

The Moravians were a religious group that left Moravia (in present-day Czechoslovakia) and settled in Germany, then started sending missionaries to the New World in the mid-1700s. They came first to Georgia, but ended up in Pennsylvania and North Carolina. Salem, founded in 1766, became a trade center where Moravian craftspeople sold their wares.

Today a tinsmith, shoemaker, weaver, dyer, potter, and cabinetmaker all work in restored shops, and bakers at the Winkler Bakery down the street turn out

Members of the Old Salem Band take a break to enjoy sugar cake made in the working 1800 Winkler Bakery.

left: *Interpreters following an 18th-century cookie recipe in the restored 1831 Vierling Wash-Bake House invite close observation.*

Members of the Old Salem Sewing Square attract as many people as any other single activity.

hundreds of loaves of bread a day, to the delight of townspeople and visitors. At Christmas time, there is increased demand for ginger cookies and love feast buns.

Walking down the streets of Old Salem puts you back in the 1700s. Everything here whispers old. The buildings are earth colors—red brick, green clapboard, and white stone with wooden beams supporting some exterior walls. One- and two-stories high, they front on Main Street and protect gardens in the back. The solid street surfaces are specially made to look like dirt. There are no traffic lights or stop signs. Instead, there are slightly raised steel ridges on the pavement marked "Stop." Old barrels with their tops cut out serve as trash cans. And the men and women who work in the shops and homes wear 18th-century costumes.

Old Salem has kept its quiet tone, and visitors pick up on it. You don't hear drivers honk or people shout here. As you walk, the only sounds are heels on the brick sidewalk, everyday greetings in soft, Southern accents, and the gentle striking of the Home Moravian Church clock every quarter hour. Though you can see the skyscrapers of downtown Winston-Salem, you firmly feel that you're back 200 years in time.

"It fascinates me what commercialism has done to Christmas," says Gene Capps, director of education and interpretation and organizer of Old Salem Christmas. "For the Moravians, Christmas was very church- and family-oriented. It was a private thing, and that's what we're trying to convey. Life and work continued as usual—that's why our crafts shops stay open. There was no time for celebration.

"It's one of the difficult things we face," says Capps. "Some visitors expect popcorn on Christmas trees and an exchange of gifts. That just didn't exist. Christmas was not a grand celebration. It was [part of] an overall picture of Moravian daily life throughout the year. Greenery was used for many holidays, not just Christmas. Moravian bands often played on the street for holidays, birthdays, and the Fourth of July. And windows were often lit with candles.

"The Moravians had a fascination with light and candlelight. They never had electric lights. They worked from sunup to sundown. Imagine these people taking resources to light a church with 20 dozen candles! We try to recreate this all."

Today's Old Salem holiday observance begins with a "Candle Tea" in early December. For two weekends, volunteers from the Women's Fellowship of Home Moravian Church dress in costume and guide visitors through the Single Brothers' House, built in 1769 as a home and workshop for single men. In the old dining room, the women demonstrate how beeswax candles were made for the Christmas Eve love feast. Five women work each shift. Early one morning, Laura Mosley pours wax into an eight-candle mold, lets it cool on the windowsill, then deftly pulls out all the candles on a string, without a break. All the while she is talking to groups of visitors.

"I've been either watching candlemaking or doing it for 70-some years," she says. "My mother used to bring me here, and I'd see one woman make all the candles for the church. Today we have many adults and children help out. They make sure the wick is in the mold, and later they measure the candle when it comes out of the mold. It has to be cut to six-and-one-half-inches."

Every 10 minutes, a new group enters to watch the candlemaking. The group has already sung carols upstairs in the Brothers' worship room to the accompaniment of an original, 1797 *Tannenberg* organ. Next the visitors go to the old kitchen for refreshments—Moravian sugar cake and coffee. Then it's down to the basement to look at the Christmas Putz (German for "decoration"), in this case a crèche.

Thousands of people return each year to the Candle Tea. "It's traditional," says Gerald Sudress, who comes with his family and friends from Greensboro, NC, "It's a good way to start off the Christmas season. My son Scott began talking about it a month ago, so there was no way we could not come."

In mid-December, the village hosts Old Salem Christmas, two days of outdoor activities including street players, Moravian brass bands, and horse-drawn wagons pulling children around the village square. Work continues inside the crafts shops, and guides talk about the labor necessary to keep the economy going through the holidays. "Matthew Miksch kept his tobacco shop open right in his home," says guide Ruby Elder. "The shop also served as a living room and bedroom. The only other room was the kitchen. Mrs. Miksch contributed to the income by making sweetmeats, gingerbread, pickles, beeswax candles, and soap."

June Drake is a guide and a shoemaker, so she loves to talk about the Shultz Shoemaker Shop. "We have Shultz's diary, and we know that he could make two or three pairs of shoes a day, with the help of an apprentice. Shoes in those days didn't have a right and a left. You just put them on any way, and they gradually molded to your feet."

The highlight of the season for many people is the love feast service at Home Moravian Church on Christmas Eve. This is a regular Moravian church service with two additions: the passing and eating of love feast buns and coffee by the congregation, and the passing of lighted candles as the choir sings. It is a singular, moving experience to which non-Moravians are invited. At the end of the love feast, everyone has met and broken bread to symbolize the brotherhood and unity of man. The candles symbolize the light of God shining in the darkness.

"When you look at all those faces illuminated, each individual illuminated, it just gets to you. The chills go up and down the spine," says Dr. Kenneth

Steaming hot cider on Salem Square.

254

IF YOU GO

For current information
on Old Salem events call
(919) 723-3688.

Music was, and is, important to Moravians and for that reason resounds through the district during special events like an Old Salem Christmas. Christmas pyramid is decorated with Bible verses, fruit, and candles.

Robinson, associate pastor at Home Moravian Church. "You feel really inspired, and you do your best to challenge people to take that light brightly shining in their faces out into the world and continue to shine."

Sharon Willis says Christmas wouldn't be the same without the love feast. "A love feast is warmth, love, soft lights, and good smells coming up from the kitchen. Everyone is happy to participate and wouldn't be anywhere else on that day. That's our Christmas. The next day is nice, opening presents. But the love feast on Christmas Eve is the most special day of the year. It's a sharing of a simple meal together in love, the agape-type meal."

On the day after Christmas, trees are taken down, ornaments put away, the Putz dismantled and stored for the next year. Full-time work resumes at Old Salem.

But the spirit of Christmas continues throughout the year, for the Moravians feel that religion was something you practice in daily life. Giving was the key to happiness—giving and love.

Old Salem gives something special to people who visit—a feeling of peace, stability, graciousness, old-world values in a new land—all things that stay with you beyond Christmas.

Photo and Map Credits (in order of appearance)

Page	Credit
Cover	Korea National Tourism Corporation
1	John Edward Young
2-5	Korea National Tourism Corporation
4	Map: Joan Forbes
6, 7	John Edward Young
8	Map: Shirley Horn
9	John Edward Young
10	Japan National Tourist Organization
12	Map: Joan Forbes
14	Betty M. Ames
16	Map: Joan Forbes
17	R. Norman Matheny
18	Christopher L. Tyner
19	Gordon N. Converse
20	Map: Joan Forbes
21	Gordon N. Converse
23	Patricia A. Taylor
24	British Tourist Authority
26	Map: Joan Forbes
28, 31, 32	Patricia A. Taylor
34	Peter Main
36, 37	British Tourist Authority
38, 40, 41	Constance E. Putnam
42	British Tourist Authority
44	Dennis Mansell
45, 46	British Tourist Authority
47	Venice Simplon-Orient-Express
48	Gayle Levee
50, 51	Map: Joan Forbes
52, 53	Gayle Levee
54, 56-58	Venice Simplon-Orient-Express
60, 61	Peter Lofthouse
62, 63	Norma Lofthouse
64	Map: Shirley Horn
66	William R. Krieger
67	E. Ditmars

68	William R. Krieger
69	E. Ditmars
70-73	Betty M. Ames
75	David H. Ahl
76	Hawaii Visitors Bureau
78	Map: Joan Forbes
79	Hawaii Visitors Bureau
80	R. Norman Matheny
82	Gayle Levee
83	John David Arms
84, 85	Mark Ragan
86	Map: Shirley Horn
87	Mark Ragan
88, 89	Tourism Australia
90	Map: Shirley Horn
91-93	Tourism Australia
94, 95	David H. Ahl
96	Map: Joan Forbes
97-99	David H. Ahl
101	Winterthur Museum and Gardens
102-106	Irish Tourist Board
108, 109	Province of British Columbia
110	Ellen Steese
110	Map: Joan Forbes
111	Province of British Columbia
112, 113	Dely Monteser Wardle
114	Map: Shirley Horn
115	Dely Monteser Wardle
116-119	Netherlands Board of Tourism
120	Map: Shirley Horn
121	Ellen Steese
122	Winterthur Museum and Gardens
124	Map: Shirley Horn
126	Winterthur Museum and Gardens
127	James Diedrick
128, 129	Pacific Princess
130	Map: Joan Forbes
131	Pacific Princess
133	Sonia W. Thomas

134, 135, 137, 138	Phyllis Krasilovsky
140	The Christian Science Monitor
142	Map: Shirley Horn
144	Deborah Taylor
146	Map: Joan Forbes
147, 148	Deborah Taylor
150, 152-155	James Diedrick
157	Florida Department of Tourism
158, 160	Catalina Cruises
162, 163	Deborah Taylor
164	Map: Joan Forbes
165, 166	Deborah Taylor
168, 169, 171	Neal Menschel
172	The Rowland Company
174	Map: Shirley Horn
175	The Rowland Company
176, 177	Florida Department of Tourism
178	Map: Joan Forbes
179	Florida Department of Tourism
181	Allen Bechky
182-184	Julia M. Johnson
184	Map: Shirley Horn
185	Julia M. Johnson
186, 187	Allen Bechky
188	Joan Wolcott Eliot
189	Allen Bechky
190	Susan Pierres
193	Map: Shirley Horn
194	Melanie Stetson Freeman
195	R. Norman Matheny
196-199	Melanie Stetson Freeman
200	Gordon N. Converse
201	Melanie Stetson Freeman
202	Colorado Tourism Board
203	Ronald R. Ruhoff, Colorado Tourism Board
204	Colorado Tourism Board
207	Melanie Stetson Freeman
208, 211	Georgiana Hamm
212	W. Gunderson, Saratoga Chamber of Commerce

214, 215, 217 Saratoga Chamber of Commerce
218-222 Gill C. Kenny, Arizona-Sonora Desert Museum
224-227 Pennsylvania Dutch Convention and Visitors Bureau
228 Map: Joan Forbes
229, 230 Pennsylvania Dutch Convention and Visitors Bureau
231 Old Salem, Inc.
232, 233 San Antonio Convention and Visitors Bureau
234 Map: Shirley Horn
235 San Antonio Convention and Visitors Bureau
236-239 Rhode Island Department of Economic Development
240-243, 245 Netherlands Board of Tourism
246 The Christian Science Monitor
247 R. Norman Matheny
248, 249 The Christian Science Monitor
250-254 Old Salem, Inc.